DELIVERED TO DECLARE

DELIVERED TO DECLARE

Gabriele Trinkle

with David Hall

HODDER AND STOUGHTON
LONDON SYDNEY AUCKLAND TORONTO

British Library Cataloguing in Publication Data

Trinkle, Gabriele
  Delivered to declare.
  1. Christian life
  I. Title   II. Hall, David
  284.4   BV4501.2

ISBN 0 340 39973 2

Hodder and Stoughton Editorial Office: 47 Bedford Square, London WC1B 3DP

This book has been dedicated in three ways: Firstly to the living God at work in his people through the sacrifice of the Lord Jesus Christ and the ministry of his Holy Spirit. Secondly to those who labour in the field setting the captives free. Finally to those precious souls who are, through much tribulation, seeing the life abundant which Jesus promised them.

CONTENTS

ACKNOWLEDGMENTS

Without the love and compassion of so many people this book would not have been written.

During three separate stages of my deliverance I received tremendous help from different groups: Mike Costello and the good people at Slade Green who took me in and identified much of my problem; John Edwards and the people of his church in Croydon who prayed and fasted until more of my past was unearthed and its effects conquered; Anita and Neville Pinto of Croydon; Jim McDonough and Walter Dettart and the John Wimber team during the Third Wave Conference, whose insight, concern and prayerful skill brought the completion of deliverance from a lifetime of occult influence. Dorothy Tucker has provided a home for me for some years for which I am grateful. Wendy Williams was an enormous encouragement during the work on this book.

And finally Peter and Mary Holmes. They have given me hope where there was none; a shoulder to cry on when I needed it most; a place of peace when I was in a turmoil; and above all have epitomised what Christian love really should be – unconditional, even during the worst moments of my life.

Gabriele Trinkle

INTRODUCTION

Ephesians 5:11 says: 'Have nothing to do with the fruitless deeds of darkness, but rather expose them.' (New International Version).

With this word from the Lord I took courage to write down my story, to expose the work of the enemy in my life. It is a story purely and simply about God's faithful love for a person he created. God loved me and wanted nothing less than to bring his salvation, healing and deliverance to me.

God is truth. He has given us his truth – his Son and his word, the Bible. As I John 3 says: Jesus came to destroy the works of the evil one.

He did this in two major ways: he died on the cross, so that our sins can be forgiven and we gain eternal life, and he cast out demons that we might gain freedom in this life.

In man's first encounter with Satan, he appeared as subtle, deceiving and destructive. Satan's tactics have not changed . . . nor are the effects less real. In man's early encounters with Jesus on earth Jesus spent much of his time teaching his disciples how to care for the whole man – in communicating salvation and combating evil.

One often-neglected aspect of this caring has been the casting out of demons. As C.S. Lewis said, there are two equally dangerous errors that we can fall into regarding demonology. One is to say that the devil and demons do not exist. The other is to have an unhealthy fascination with it (*Screwtape Letters*).

It seems, today, that we are seeing both. Generally in the church, people do not believe in the demonic and in the world there is an unhealthy fascination with it.

Our society is entrenched in the supernatural or paranormal. It draws people like a magnet, stimulating their minds with the hope of immortality and power. Many today have been brought up on a diet of science-fiction and the supernatural through books and television, watered down with the belief that satanism, witchcraft and the like went out with the Middle Ages. The fact that in England the Witchcraft Act was repealed in the middle of this century as obsolete is considered an indication of how enlightened we have become! Coupled with this is the destruction of whole societies being brought about by the drug sub-culture, cries of free expression and general unrest, both in families and nations. These are also motivated by the same demonic realm.

It is hoped that this book will speak to you and in some small way enable you to obey the commission of Jesus fully – to cast out demons, to heal the sick and to preach the Good News of the kingdom of God. (Matthew 10:1).

Also I hope it may speak to those who are outside the life of Christ, or who have been involved in the occult, to those who are troubled and tormented by demons – there *is* freedom in the mighty name of Jesus Christ.

As John 8:36 says: 'those whom the Son sets free shall be *free indeed.*'

1

SOLD TO SATAN

The six-month-old baby wriggled. She lay naked on a cloth-covered table. A middle-aged woman leaned over the child, touching as she did so the point of a knife with her forefinger to make certain it was sharp. Satisfying herself that it was, she grabbed the tiny ankle kicking away on the dark cloth.

A whimper left the young throat as blood spurted from a nick in the small heel.

Mysterious guttural incantations came from the woman's throat. Her ceremony was almost over. The child had been bound to Satan by a blood-tie. A foundation was laid for a life in bondage and sickness.

A sudden gust of wind at the window flickered the curtains open and brought a flash of light into the darkened first-floor room. The woman lifted the child from the table, dressed it and returned it to the mother. Neither mother nor child understood the power that had been present. But both would live to regret its invocation; the former as a mother, the latter as its victim.

Four years later the same child was taken to be shown off to another relative. This aunt was rich. In the luxury of a huge sitting room with deep, soft furniture, they relaxed. The aunt persuaded the mother, who did not know what was involved, that a 'small ceremony' would be 'good for the child'.

A beige curtain covered one end of the room. The mother gave up her child and left as the youngster was taken behind the curtain. Again the child was stripped naked. Every intimate part of her body was touched in the black-magic ceremony which married her to Satan – a tiny, innocent bride and a malevolent bridegroom.

But again it was a bestial ceremony, unspeakable. In years to come only the merciful interventions of blackouts and loss of memory would prevent the girl from digging into the recesses of her mind to re-live the awful session behind the curtain. All she would remember was the woman dressed in black and a strange man adding his presence to the sick and depraved operation.

The memory might be faint, but the effects of that torture to the body, soul and spirit would blight the life of that child for years, even into adulthood.

I know. It was my life.

2

THE EVIL TAKES ROOT

I was born in Bamberg, Germany, as the church bells announced it was fifteen minutes past eleven on a Sunday morning. My mother, a beautiful woman, hardly knew the birth had taken place she was so free from pain.

We lived at the very edge of the town in an impressive house which we were fortunate to have. At the end of the war in Germany houses were difficult to obtain and the only reason we were given this was because my aunt had married an American officer and allowed us to live with them.

It was a crowded home with Aunt Hildegaard and Uncle Dick; their children Barbara (aged five) and Katy (four); my mother and father and myself, an only child and destined for a very different life from that of which my parents dreamed.

My mother was tall, blonde and radiantly attractive. Her name was Maria and I adored her. A fashion model before her marriage, she had also been a ballroom dancer, and an athlete. It seemed that she could do anything she wanted. Success accompanied her pleasure-filled life. As a gymnast she had starred in the dancing display which was the overture to the 1936 Olympic Games in Berlin. Only days before she had thrown away the chance to run in the Olympics: leading the field in her race she decided she had had enough and simply ran off the track. Her trainers were so amazed one flung his stopwatch into the arena in disgust. That disappointed coach was Max Trinkle, the man she had married a year before. He was tall, dark-haired and had a strong temper. He was furious now. She didn't seem to care and it was an attitude he couldn't cope with. And he failed to cope with it in later years.

An Olympic trainer – proficient in many different skills – my father lived for sport. The early 1930s were the high points of his life, since Hitler encouraged sport so much. Even the start of the war didn't reduce his enthusiasm, as he became a physical instructor in the army.

At the end of the war he was a broken man. It wasn't just defeat. Being forced first to fight, and then to live as a prisoner-of-war in America, had built up hatred inside him and made him angry with the world.

Germany was picking up the pieces after the Allied victory when my parents met again. My mother was fleeing from the east where the Russians were already exerting their victorious influence and my father was making his stumbling way home from America. They met on a railway station – a sad meeting since my father discovered then that the son mother had conceived while he was on leave a couple of years before had died at two months old.

The despondent couple made for the house in Bamberg and the relatives who were willing to share their home.

The town itself was situated in a valley surrounded by forest and hills. Our house was perched on a hill which dropped away into the valley in which nestled the town centre, dominated by the dome of the Catholic cathedral. The forty Roman Catholic churches swamped the lone Protestant rival and nuns and priests seemed at times to be the only occupants of the streets. The forest where my father loved to hunt was just a few hundred yards from our back door; a river meandered along between our home and the towering trees. It was a lovely place to be a little girl, the replacement child for the son who had not lived.

In fact I was the result of their reunion. Nine months after they found their way to Bamberg I was born.

I was a sickly child. What we did not know then was that the aunt who had performed that ceremony had invited the Devil to make me constantly ill and charmed sickness and disease into my body to render me dependent on her and my mother.

My illnesses were all the more worrying because although many people in Germany went hungry after the war we did not. Father had managed to get a job with a local electronics company dealing in kitchen equipment and would often go hunting with the owner of the company who lived in the same street. They brought home rabbits, deer and even wild boar. I remember father returning home on one occasion with a deer hanging over his shoulder for mother to cut up, cook and serve.

I had no real relationship with him. I never called him father, simply Atz, his nickname. I hated him without knowing why and he didn't seem to care. Disappointment that I was a girl, and not the sporting son he wanted, seemed to create a gulf between us.

He desperately wanted me to excel, but did not perceive the need to build first a secure foundation of trust. When I was four we were on a pleasure boat on a large lake when he threw me overboard and told me to swim. As I thrashed about in the water, squealing and petrified, he ordered other people away when they wanted to jump in to help. I was made to flap my terrified way back to the shore, the seeds of hate against my father taking root. His violent temper didn't help either, nor the fact that he started drinking. These led to a number of frightening clashes. Like a volcano waiting to erupt, he simmered. Then one word would set him off. On one occasion the wrong word sent him into the bathroom in a rage, smashing the mirror on the wall, perfume bottles and other oddments.

Three years after my parents moved into the house my aunt and uncle and their children left. Then the owners of the house who had been driven out during the war were allowed back to share their home with us – three old ladies. One was a headmistress and another a teacher in a local school. They wore dark clothes, always looked sombre, and rarely smiled. Life took on a grim appearance for a lively three-year-old like myself. I wasn't allowed to make a noise and something dark and oppressive dominated the building.

If the aunt who had ushered occult practices into the house

had left, the evil presence and influence lived on. But it was not acknowledged for to mother the occult was never real, it was something to laugh at; 'harmless fun' she called it all. She had angered her relatives years before as a teenager hiding under a table before a seance. They didn't know she was there until she bounded out from under the table at a critical part of the seance. They screamed and drove her from the room.

Although mother had a circle of very respectable friends she seemed also to be drawn to people with interests in the occult. She visited a fortune teller and was given charms for the house. Her 'fun' view of it all spilled over into our home. On one wall, for example, she hung a picture frame – with no picture inside. Mother would smile at me in her charming way and say: 'Can't you see the picture?' I never could. All I could see was wallpaper through the glass in the centre of the frame.

But I could see other things – and they frightened me. As a baby my cot was in my parents' room and as I grew, afraid to sleep alone, I slept in a room with my mother – no problem for her since the rift between her and father meant they slept apart.

When I was alone in a room, tucked away under the angled eaves, or in other parts of the house, I could hear sounds: sounds I couldn't identify. There would be knocking noises. Black shapes would flit in front of my eyes as if taunting me. It was mysterious ... mystical ... and altogether too much for a little girl.

But when I spoke of these experiences my mother simply laughed. 'You imagined it,' she said. This lack of belief in my assertions hurt and frightened me, forcing me to withdraw further into my own world. Easygoing as she was, I could never quite work out if mother liked to frighten me. One Christmas she made an advent calendar; a pretty picture, with little doors cut into the cardboard so that I could open a different door each day and reveal an object. There was a ball, a little picture of baby Jesus, and a Christmas tree. But on one side of the calendar was the huge figure of a devil – a horrible caricature which had no part in the Christmas story.

It was another of mother's jokes. I was scared of the devil. When it was time to open a door I refused and mother would have to argue before I would reluctantly go near the hateful figure and pull the appropriate door open.

All the while, the power of the evil spirits which had been implanted into me, was growing, and with it the effects of many curses which had been put on me through the family tree – a legacy of generations before. As I discovered years later, for generations members of the family had become deeply involved in the occult, giving themselves to fortune telling, analysing dreams, divination, witchcraft, black and white magic, and even to the depths of satanism.

When I was a few months old, I was so weak doctors thought I would die. I had an inflammation in both ears which led to giddy spells as I grew older. At the age of five I had health problems of a different kind. Running into the house from the garden one sunny afternoon I couldn't climb the twelve steps into the kitchen. I collapsed in a heap and mother rushed me to the doctor.

The strength had gone from my legs, so they were encased in plaster in an effort to strengthen them – not pleasant on a warm, sunny afternoon for a young girl. Eventually diphtheria was diagnosed. Because that was so severe and I was being treated for it I couldn't have the usual childhood innoculations and consequently got more than my fair share of all the ailments that went round the town.

I missed the first year at school when I was six through the after-effects of the diphtheria, and polio which by now had also been diagnosed. I was fortunate that the headmistress in whose house we were living gave me books and private tuition. I enjoyed learning. Sitting in the garden under the trees, cuddling a rag doll, I had also been given an understanding of illness and used to think and dream. I would often take a pair of scissors to my doll and open her up for an operation, leaving mother to stitch my handiwork back together again when I was asleep.

Although the polio I had was only a mild form it confined me to bed for some months and the inactivity, plus the medication, turned my childish frame into a tubby hormone-imbalanced body that would give me a lifetime of weight problems.

All the while – despite my youth – I knew something was wrong. I was so different from my mother. She was full of fun, enthusiastic, athletic . . . I was fat, serious and a failure at anything that required energy or dexterity. It was that kind of despondency that led me to run away one day with my rag doll clutched tightly in my chubby arms.

They discovered my hiding place in the fields and father beat me and threatened worse next time. I felt I could never be happy. In fact I was smacked often – generally for what I considered flimsy reasons.

It may seem strange to someone with a more normal childhood but an awareness of demons and evil was always with me. Consequently I was desperately afraid of being alone. Mother would look under my bed to allay my fears and soothe me with: 'You see, there's nothing there.' But I knew, deep down I knew, something was present . . . something wicked.

Father refused to believe that a child of his could be so scared, so one evening he took mother out for a walk after threatening me with the worst beating of my life if I left the room. They would only be away thirty minutes, he promised. Within seconds of their leaving it started: the curtains twitched; the door handle turned slowly on its own; black shapes flitted across my vision and there were blurred noises, creaking and the long screech of an owl from the nearby forest. I was petrified and ran from the house, preferring the promised beating to the noises and movements.

When my parents returned half an hour later it was to find me cowering in a neighbour's house. The beating simply fuelled my hatred for my father. He was such a huge figure and I was so small. How brave he was to hit me!

Occasionally, however, he tried to give me pleasant surprises. Sometimes he would bring me sweets. One evening I remember he returned with some beautiful chocolate eggs filled with cream. They were placed carefully on a table ready for me to select and eat one before going to bed. Within seconds one word from mother had started an angry scene which ended with father flinging the eggs at mother and splattering them all over the wallpaper. Tears streamed down my face as I licked at the wallpaper trying to get every drop of the cream.

My mother was my life. I rarely left her side. I was probably the first thing she had ever seriously been concerned for. Just occasionally I would go to church on my own, some deep desire within me overcoming the fear of the long walk into the town.

One influence had captured my young spirit; that of a nun. For a few weeks while my mother was ill my father's boss paid a nun from the town to come and look after us. Her soothing spirit seemed to bring a peace I did not know existed, freeing me from my nightly noises and shapes. Even as a child I recognised there was good, and a light which could conquer the darkness of my visions. I was determined to become a nun.

3

SICKNESS AND DRUGS

It was not until I was thirteen that life really began for me. We moved to Asperg, a small town near Stuttgart where my father had a similar job to his previous one – involved with electrical appliances for kitchens. The job had one exciting side benefit for me: the boss owned a cinema in the town and we were given a flat on top of it in which to live. It was a large flat with four big rooms but the real blessing was that I was allowed to go to the cinema whenever I wanted without paying. Of course it meant that I watched anything . . .

Still anxious to please my parents I tried swimming. The previous few years had demonstrated that I was a failure at gymnastics and athletic sports but I considered swimming was a different matter. Within a year I began to swim seriously, practising hard – up to six hours a day – before and after school while my friends did my maths, German and English homework. I didn't tell my father. This was to be my gift to him – an achievement without his help.

Again I failed. My chubby little body just wouldn't move through the water fast enough for my spirit. It was a bitter disappointment, so much so that I decided to end my life. For an hour after a swimming contest in which I had again failed to win I wandered along the pavement trying to pluck up courage to jump in front of a car. I lacked even the courage to do that.

After the long journey home I cried bitterly and raced up the wooden stairs alongside the cinema into the flat. My parents were out and I went into father's room to his desk on which lay a knife. The silver decoration on the wooden handle had always fascinated me; now I wanted it for a purpose other than ornamental. I slipped the hunting knife from its leather sheath and sat on the floor with my back pressed into the desk. I peeled back the sleeves of my dress which hung over my wrist and paused momentarily, examining the pink flesh and the bluish veins spreading up my arm.

I slashed the knife downwards, quickly transferring it to the other hand and repeating the process on my other wrist. The sticky blood felt like treacle as it began to dribble over my hands.

I became frightened and confused; waves of nausea enveloped me and I staggered to the bathroom. As my senses returned the blood began to dry and the bleeding stopped. My wrists had cut-marks on them but little more than the scratches I had received from holiday fruit-picking. I had failed again – another thing I couldn't do properly.

I felt a sense of disgust at myself, though whether it was for what I had tried to do, or the revelation of failure, I didn't know. Shakily I took a roll of bandage from the bathroom cabinet and carefully wound a length round my wrists, covering the scratches and yet ensuring the white bandage would not be seen under the sleeves of my dress.

Evil still dogged me... and the ever present fear of the moving shapes, voices and noises in my home led me to the conclusion that I was destined to a life of fear. The sort of films I watched – love stories, horror movies – did nothing to ease the situation.

Just once my father used his physical strength to defend me when I was afraid. I was taking my little dachshund, Bazi, for a walk one dark evening when some youths grabbed the leash, dragged the dog away and began to molest me. Father happened to be looking for me, saw what was happening and rushed to my defence. Ironically he was badly beaten as a youth ripped off a piece of fence and hit him. Only when my mother appeared and flung her bunch of keys at one of the lads, splitting his face open, did they run off.

It was the first time I began to sense that my father wasn't the big strong he-man I imagined him to be. And my mother perplexed me with her speed and strength – very different from the love and affection she was always showering on me.

Another incident during the school holiday confused me even more, when I considered their reactions. I was working in an open-air swimming pool as a Red Cross helper. At the end of the day four men who helped in our first aid team pulled me down and pressed an ether-soaked pad on my face. I kicked and screamed until the powerful fumes thrust me into oblivion. When I came to I was in an ambulance being taken home. The men had warned me not to talk about the incident but mother smelt the anaesthetic and, after questioning me, called the police. I was made to have embarrassing medical checks, questioned for what seemed like hours by police officers, and the men were fined. At the time I deeply resented my parents putting me through such torment – my punishment seemed far worse than that of the four perpetrators.

At sixteen I left school for college to train as a doctor's receptionist. It was a six-month course which fascinated me. Laboratory work, medical training and other aspects of the work were interesting and seemed to open up a new future.

It was my father who took care of my first job. He arranged for me to go for an interview with a doctor for a position as receptionist. The doctor was tall, blond, and good-looking. His white coat gave him an air of authority as he looked across his desk at me. I felt self-conscious, an overweight teenager with few qualifications, keen to start work. But I got the job. The surgery had about fifteen rooms including an X-ray department and physiotherapy unit.

I was told to spend the first few days watching what the other nurses did and followed after them like a shadow, keenly observing everything that was done. Eventually I moved into the physiotherapy unit and discovered work which gave me a real pleasure. There was something satisfying about helping people and I soon acquired some skill at giving massage and injections.

The polio I had suffered as a child had left me with a weakened back and I often had pain in my back, hips and legs. I had also begun to have trouble from gall-stones – an unusual thing in someone of my age but dreadfully painful and, I am positive, the result of that childhood curse.

I was taking various tablets for my pain – librium, valium and atrophine and now I began to play with morphine. My different ailments, plus the drugs, only combined to wreak further havoc on my health.

Eventually I needed a gall-bladder operation, having already had operations to remove my appendix and tonsils and a growth in my throat when I was younger. It seemed hospital life was to be my future – on both sides of the blanket.

On my eighteenth birthday I had the gall-bladder operation. It should have been simple in someone of my age but it wasn't. When I finally came round after the operation the surgeons admitted I had nearly died. Oxygen had been rushed to me and I suffered from the trauma of it for weeks.

When I eventually returned to work it was to join another doctor – still in orthopaedics. It was something of a miracle appointment and marked my first real contact with Christianity since my childhood dreams of becoming a nun.

Out of work after the operation I was waiting miserably on the railway station to catch a train to the job centre in Ludwigsburg when a girl approached me.

'You don't look very happy,' she remarked.

I explained that I was looking for a job.

'What do you do?' she asked.

As soon as I had told her a smile spread across her face. She was a receptionist in a surgery and her boss was looking for a new nurse. Ursula, that was her name, took me straight to the surgery. During the journey she told me about Jesus Christ and how he had changed her life. She felt our meeting was a 'divine intervention'. I wasn't so sure.

The doctor was friendly and the set-up certainly offered me the sort of experience I wanted even though it was smaller than my previous workplace, being an extension to the doctor's flat. The smallness of it – and the doctor's wife – put me off.

I could sense the wife's antagonism immediately he introduced us after my interview. She seemed to want to protect him – although why she should be worried about me I couldn't imagine.

As the doctor shook my hand he made it clear the job was mine.

'No thank you,' I told him. 'I don't think I want it.' All I would do was promise to call back in a day or two if I changed my mind.

Ursula was quite shocked. Obviously it wouldn't occur to a Christian such as her to go for the interview and not take the job. But what did she know about life! As I closed the door behind me I could see the disappointment written across her face.

That night I wrestled with the dilemma: should I take the job? I knew I would hate the doctor's wife; I knew Ursula would try and trap me into religion... yet inside a day I telephoned and agreed to start the following week. I don't know what made me do it.

She seemed, to me, to be a strange girl. Her hair was lashed in a tight bun on the back of her head. Old-fashioned clothes and shoes meant I could have predicted she was a Christian – dull and uninteresting. And yet she was different. She had a joy in her face that didn't seem real. She was friendly and in all my eighteen years I had never really made friends with anyone.

Somehow my antagonism towards her message didn't seem to matter. I also liked her parents, who were a happy couple constantly chattering to each other – unlike my parents who often spoke to each other through me when they wanted to break the ominous silence.

I laughed when Ursula told me Jesus loved me and, although I could tell my reaction made her sad, she didn't argue. I was deliberately mean, testing her friendship often, without finding her failing me. Amazing!

It was probably the calm way she reacted to my cynicism that eventually encouraged me to go to church. Ursula had invited me to the Christmas service at the Methodist church she went to. I told her I would not be going. 'There are more exciting things to do at Christmas,' I boasted, knowing inside that I would probably do nothing but sit at home and listen to Mother and Father row, or find myself being picked on by one or the other at the slightest provocation.

But I went, on my own, creeping into the back of the little church that smelt of varnish and polish. I slithered into a seat and stared at the front, ignoring the faces that twisted questioningly in my direction. Ursula was near the front. I could see the back of her head, the tight bun bobbing as she sang, but she was not aware I was at the service. I knew I could leave without her even knowing I was there. That gave me a mocking pleasure. It wasn't to be, however.

As the service wound on its turgid way the minister leaned over his pulpit and looked across the congregation of about fifty. 'We shall take our Christmas, Bible promises as a guide for the next year,' he said. I wondered what he meant. But then, it was no more mysterious than a lot of the things they did in church.

The meaning soon became clear. A bucket-like box was being handed along each row and everyone was expected to take from it one of the small motto cards packing it, like draw tickets in a sweepstake.

'What a pathetic thing to do,' I muttered. 'Who needs a promise from a dead book?' But I took one of the little crumpled papers and untwisted it to read what it said. I grinned to myself as I read it and almost laughed out loud. It was ridiculous, confirming my belief that the Bible was all mumbo-jumbo and had no place in the life of an intelligent person.

My silent mirth was cut short with the minister's next few words. 'In our usual fashion we'll each read out our promise,' he said, reading his in a bold voice that injected some power into the verse I would not have credited it could have. And then the congregation started standing, one at a time, reading out their individual verses. Even that would not have been so bad, but they did it one after the other in neat rows – and worked their way back towards me.

What was I to do? The woman next to me made my decision for me. She stood, read her verse out, sat down and turned straight to me with a look that indicated it was my turn.

I stood, hating every second of it. Smoothing out the
paper between my trembling fingers I read: 'I consider that
our present sufferings are not worth comparing with the
glory that will be revealed in us.' (Romans 8:18, New
International Version).

As my voice rang out there was an audible gasp and,
although I was reading the verse and deliberately staring at
the paper, I knew Ursula had recognised my voice. I was
embarrassed and angry with myself for going to the church.
Sitting down on the old wooden seat, I stared at the minister
and glowered at anyone who dared to look at me.

The meeting confirmed all my suspicions about church.
The music was provided by an elderly woman pumping
ridiculously away with her feet at an ancient harmonium. I
could count the number of young people on one hand – the
rest were elderly men and women. Ursula's bun was
obviously standard style for the women; most of them wore
their hair in that fashion. I remembered what we had always
called them when I was younger – 'hallelujah onions'. That
recollection cheered me slightly.

When the service ended Ursula rushed back towards me.
There was no escape, and little point since she now knew I
was there. Her next action took me by surprise, though. She
handed me a neatly packaged present. She was either
hedging her bets or had some idea that I would come.

I took the gift and thanked her. Perhaps it would make it a
worthwhile evening after all, I thought.

I clutched the little package like a child as I made my way
through the streets past shops decorated for Christmas. At
home I carefully snipped through the ribbon and teased
away the pretty paper to reveal the gift. A New Testament!
Die Gute Nachricht – the New Testament in modern
German. My disappointment was bitter. I had not known
what to expect – but this was certainly not even on my list of
possibilities. It was another of Ursula's naïve moves to make
me a Christian. I hated it. I felt the pressure. I sat on my bed
angry at the present and yet angry at myself for despising it,
and I was aware of a stirring within me – a malicious glee
pervading my body.

I determined it would be years before I went back to church.

In fact it wasn't long. Some time later I agreed to go to a youth meeting – it didn't seem as threatening as a church service, and Ursula was still one of the only friends I had. For a couple of years I went to those particular evenings but mainly for one reason: one of the youth leaders, Manfred, was so good-looking! Fair-haired, tall, and with a gentle voice, I always felt safe when he was there.

On one occasion I even pretended to become a Christian, making my way to the front of the church when there was an altar call, to impress Manfred. The young people were delighted. Inside I was chuckling with glee – what idiots they were. They believed anything.

That decision gave them pleasure – but it brought me some problems. I was often told off for wearing make-up; they called it 'being worldly'.

Ursula saw through my false decision very quickly. And as she began to increase the pressure on me to be a real Christian something inside me began to rebel. I was under pressure from another quarter too; my work was suffering because the attitude of the doctor's wife was becoming more and more unbearable. Life seemed utterly miserable.

When I was alone the dark shapes and noises were almost more than I could endure and my gall-stones were giving me more pain than ever, despite the operation.

A university clinic in Munich failed to cure me and depression set in as I lay recuperating for some weeks in the white, metal-framed, hospital bed. The whole world was an empty void.

Ursula, of course, wouldn't give up. As I lay in torment one night my door opened and a nurse ushered a man into the room. 'This is your pastor,' she explained. 'He's come to see you.'

I was doped with drugs and could hardly concentrate. I gathered he was a local Methodist minister who was a friend of Ursula and she had contacted him and asked him to visit me.

His words drifted over me. I recall he prayed at one point

but nothing happened. There was no visitation from God; no soothing hand. As he left the pastor casually placed a book on my bedside table. 'Read this. I am sure you will find it interesting,' he commented.

When I saw the title the following morning I almost tipped it into the bin. *The Cross and the Switchblade.* So obviously Christian. The man hadn't any tact.

Life was intolerable and I sank lower and lower into the pit of depression and pain despite the drugs which gave me some relief. Eventually I was sent to a sanatorium in the southern countryside.

The peace of the Alpine mountains and the green rich hills which stretched into the distance should have helped ease my mind. They didn't. The shadowy black shapes, noises in my room, and frightening apparitions which had dogged my footsteps all my life were now coming with terrifying regularity. I hated to be left alone. My room became a cell in which the demons tormented me and drove me nearer to the edge of the black abyss.

I had read all the books in my mini-library when I discovered *The Cross and the Switchblade* – somehow it had travelled with me. An avid reader, I flicked through the first few pages. As I did so I was gripped. I saw the life of a young preacher radically changed when he began to follow God's call. I read of the miracles that happened among street gangs as he simply reached out in God's love to the roughest, toughest teenagers in New York. It began to dawn on me what I was missing. Life for me was always black but the darkness of my visions need not always haunt me. There was a light side – God.

The psychiatrists at the sanatorium did not agree. 'You have a problem with life. You must get out and enjoy yourself more,' one young doctor told me. When I admitted I had never kissed a boy he gave me his prescription: 'Go to the local dance. Be happy. Don't be so afraid of men.'

He looked pityingly at me. His white coat gleamed in the dismal single room. When he had gone I looked at the table, desk and wardrobe which made up the furnishing. A sink and shower in opposite corners were the only other items to break the monotony. Again even the view from the window seemed drab – green fields, green trees, green hedges, and white-capped mountains. It was so boring! I couldn't face it any longer. But as I became aware of this, I realised something else: I couldn't face going home either.

For the first time I began to see that something about my home was influencing me; and not for good. True, my parents had paid for my school, my training and my treatment, but real love was a word that wasn't understood, and there was something else that wasn't right that I couldn't put my finger on. The memory of the strange things which had happened when I was a young child came dimly to mind. More shadowy figures and a frightening creak that I knew only I could hear jerked me back into the present.

I needed to get away. But where to?

In a letter Ursula had mentioned England and a friend who had gone to be an au pair. I wrote to Ursula and got the address of the place where the girl had worked – Clarendon School, Kinmel in North Wales. I would write.

It was a boarding school with many of the children coming from missionary families. My letter was answered by return. They offered me a job. I didn't need the sanatorium or my home. I would go to England, or rather, Wales.

My parents hated the idea.

'Think of all the training you have had. You can't throw it away to be an au pair. And, in England . . .' father shouted.

Mother simply sat on the other side of the room sobbing. But I was adamant. I was going.

Eventually they agreed to my going and, when the day of my departure arrived, father even offered to take me to the station. It was a grudging offer but I accepted, especially since it was snowing outside. The journey was as silent as the drifting snowflakes. Mother sat in the back of the car crying into her handkerchief. I heard the occasional word . . . 'wasted life' . . . 'all we've done' . . . 'ungrateful' . . . Father sat upright at the wheel staring ahead through the swinging windscreen wiper, saying nothing. The journey took twice as

long as usual because of the weather but eventually father
eased the car into a parking space in front of the station in
Stuttgart.

My train left at midnight – a few minutes away. Mother
grabbed the suitcases I had packed and shuffled towards the
barrier, with me following. Acting with all the boldness I
could muster I pushed my way into a carriage, crashed the
suitcases on to the luggage rack and returned to the door to
say goodbye to mother again. We hugged each other and
kept repeating 'goodbye'.

Tears flooded down her face. 'You won't like it,' she
forecast. 'You'll be back. There is still time to change your
mind.'

I had heard the arguments before. Again I ignored them.
The train began to move and I watched as she vanished into
the distance, a sad woman waving a soggy handkerchief and
whispering: 'You'll be back.'

It would be a long time before I would return.

4

HUNTING FOR FREEDOM

As I made my way back to the seat I had already reserved by leaving my round shoulder bag propped up against the corner of the compartment, I rubbed my own red eyes and tried not to let the other occupants see I had been crying.

My three fellow passengers were all men. It was a few minutes before I realised that they were also all English. For a while I tried to work out what they were saying but they spoke too quickly. Eventually, however, they began to talk to me, slowly and loudly – as if I were deaf. I didn't mind, the companionship was better than the hours of boredom I had believed were ahead of me. My English was rusty but if I was going to be in a school with hundreds of children it was good practice. Every now and then the ticket collector would peep round the door and grin at me, mumbling in German: 'Is everything all right?' I nodded. Mother had made a point of asking him to keep an eye on me. He was a cheery fellow with a beaming red face so it was good to know he was keeping his promise.

I was quite safe though. The Englishmen were exactly how I imagined Englishmen to be – except for the lack of bowler hats and rolled umbrellas. They all wore dark suits, and carried briefcases, which they opened occasionally to pass a paper round when they were talking business. They bought me a drink and a sandwich when the refreshment trolley came along, and I began to think my first journey alone outside Germany was not going to be too bad.

I smiled to myself because the trio decided to be father figures and, since my own father had spent his time trying to dissuade me from going to England, it was good to know

someone English cared. 'Don't talk to strangers,' they
warned, three men who had been perfect strangers
themselves until a few hours before. I was advised not to 'go
with anyone' and even with my shortage of English it was
evident what they meant.

As our train neared Ostend I imagined what it would be
like to actually be on my own. Even that wasn't to be – yet.
The gentlemanly trio took me under their wings escorting me
from the train to the ferry and, because they were going to
Victoria, made certain that I stuck with them.

I was ushered along like a child, but despite being nearly
twenty I was not unhappy with the arrangement.

The train to London was not at all like the German one. In
Germany the compartments were larger and more roomy,
now suddenly we were cramped into a little cubby-hole with
two other passengers. The seats were not as comfortable,
either. Still my friends made sure I sat next to the window
and pointed out the features of the countryside although it
didn't look a great deal different from Germany.

When we arrived at Victoria my guides insisted on taking
me by taxi to Euston for my change of train – and were very
apologetic that they were not to join me on the next stage of
my journey. I thought of taking their names and addresses to
write a thank-you card but imagined what their wives would
think, and decided it was not the most prudent thing to do.
Instead I jostled my way through the milling crowds at
Euston to discover I had a few minutes to find the correct
platform for the last lap of my journey, Prestatyn! Even the
spelling of that name seemed unusual.

For what seemed like an eternity – actually about five
hours – we chuntered towards Wales. I was worried about
missing the station and every time the train slowed down
stared out of the window frantically to make certain I did not
stay on too long.

Eventually the name Prestatyn showed up. I grabbed my
two suitcases and round shoulder bag – all I now owned –
and struggled on to the platform. Fortunately the messages
which had gone backwards and forwards from the school
had all got through – a driver was waiting to collect me. He

spoke very little and when he did I understood little. His speech was hard to follow – he was very Welsh. Until then it hadn't really sunk in that Wales wasn't England. Geography lessons were one thing – being there was another.

The journey was eerie. It was after midnight, dark with a half-moon glowing behind moving clouds. My driver did tell me not to be afraid – I guessed he had picked up other au pairs before and realised something of what we were going through. Trees, hedges, and houses flashed by, illuminated for fractions of a second by the car's headlights as we sped on. It was only a twenty minute journey but it seemed like hours before the car swung off the road between two brick pillars.

We drove along a bumpy track of a road with a fence on either side. Suddenly the car swung round almost in a complete circle and my driver spoke: 'There we are. Clarendon School.'

The moon's ghostly white light illuminated the iron gate, huge pillars on either side of it, a forecourt, and then the building – huge, turreted like a medieval castle. He swung the vehicle to a halt on the gravelly drive and helped me out, taking my cases and leaving me to carry my shoulder bag.

I pushed open the huge oak doors and stood gasping in an enormous entrance hall. Ahead was a staircase that wound up to the left out of sight. The entrance hall was sunken, with other rooms leading off a passage opposite the entrance door. I was afraid.

'Come on,' the driver said. 'Let's get a drink and I'll show you your room.'

He marched across the lobby, up the three steps on the other side and I followed meekly as he led me to the kitchen. I drank a welcome cup of tea – the English drink I was told – before he dropped the cups into the sink and grabbed my bags again.

Back into the lobby area he walked a short distance down the main passage and pressed a button on the wall. I had not really had time to notice the lift before, but creaking and groaning the lift cage appeared as two metal doors clanged open. I stepped inside and as the driver followed he smashed the doors together, pressed the button for the top floor and lectured me on always closing the lift doors – 'It won't move unless you do,' he warned.

Before I could nod my understanding the lift lurched to a halt. I staggered against him and kicked over a suitcase. The driver (I later learned he was the school porter) muttered under his breath and jabbed his finger into the display of buttons on the wall. Still nothing happened. All I could see was a collection of unpainted bricks on the other side of the grille door of the lift cage. My heart began to beat furiously. What was happening?

By now the porter was shouting for help. His voice echoed through the cell that the lift had become, and bounced back off the bare walls.

After five minutes or so voices answered. 'We're all right now, luv,' he said, turning to me. 'Soon be out and tucked up in bed.'

But it was another thirty minutes before the lift squeaked its way upwards and the gates crashed open.

Frightened and unhappy I had more stairs to climb – a winding staircase right into the attic of the huge building. Then I followed the porter down a narrow passage past four doors, which I gathered from his whispers housed other girls, to the end of the passage. He opened the door and stepped back to allow me to enter. He had to – there was only room for one, a bed and a chair. As the door closed behind the porter, I clambered round my suitcases, filling up the available floor area, and undressed, laying my clothes on the chair. I didn't even wash – I was so tired. I flung myself on to the bed and wept. Tired as I was my mind refused to sleep. I watched the sky gradually lighten through the thin curtains until sun streamed in on me. Only then did I drag myself to my feet and perch on the edge of the bed to peep out of the window. I looked across the roof – my room was in a sort of turret – and saw in the distance the sea, a wishy-washy grey colour. Between the school and the sea was nothing but green trees and fields, punctuated by white blobs – sheep grazing. It was beautiful; but inside I was still feeling afraid. Something wasn't right and I hoped desperately that it was only my nerves reacting to my first night in a foreign country.

Hardly had I taken in the view when there was a knock on the door.

A German voice called out: 'Can I come in?'

What a relief. Someone to whom I could talk. Another au pair had come to show me the bathroom, where to hang my clothes, and then take me to breakfast... and to work.

Back down the winding staircase we dragged the suitcases and I was directed to a room with wardrobes inside. I was given space in one and a few drawers in a chest-of-drawers. My clothes were quickly stuffed away and the suitcases left for the porter to hide somewhere in the attic.

After washing I felt a little fresher and was taken back downstairs realising that we had not used the lift but the main staircase. We turned straight round at the foot of the stairs and entered the kitchen where half-a-dozen girls were already at work. I sat at an enormous table and ate a bowl of cereal and crunched some overdone toast. Then I was told to follow the German-speaking girl around for a day or two and help her, at the same time 'learning the ropes'. What a strange expression! There were no ropes!

One of the girls came from Switzerland, but I can't recall the nationality of the others. All I do know is that they were fairly unanimous in their dislike of the school. In its heyday, the late 1950s and early 1960s, there were two hundred and twenty girls and thirty staff. But by now Clarendon School was feeling the financial pressure which had already closed a number of boarding schools and it was difficult to attract domestic staff.

It was also Christian!

Many of the girls were the daughters of missionaries; one of the grand-daughters of the Emperor Haile Selassie was there. And we eight au pairs seemed to do everything. We cleaned, changed beds, cooked, washed up and ran errands. When we did get free time there was nothing to do with it. The school was several miles from the nearest town – too far to walk – and there was no bus route. We were isolated.

To pass the time I did a Cambridge University certificate

in English, going to Bangor University to pass the final examination.

We weren't allowed to drink or smoke and the drugs I had become used to taking before leaving Germany were obviously frowned on. I followed the example of some of the other au pairs and created places to hide my 'valuables'. The best place for my bottle of Scotch, I discovered, was behind my bulky German Bible and the English Bible they liked us to use. Cigarettes and my drugs fitted neatly on to the shelf behind the same camouflage.

When I had some free time I would sit in front of the open window and light a cigarette, blowing the smoke carefully out of the room, over the roof; enjoying the habit but keen not to be found out. There was also a heavy market in the little village shop for mints to disguise the smell of our breath after drinking.

My friends, I discovered, had made their own arrangements for entertainment in the absence of television, or even radio. I was invited into one of the girls' rooms one afternoon during a rest period.

They crowded round the bed, some of us perched on it, while one of the girls held a piece of string with a needle on the end, dangling it in the air. One after another they asked it a question – usually something silly like: 'Will my husband be good-looking?' The needle was uncanny; it swung one way for 'yes' and the other for 'no'. I watched the hand of the girl holding it and there was no way she was manipulating it. The questions got more serious and I became scared. Suddenly, bearing in mind all my visions and noises, I knew it was evil. I left them to it, perhaps one of the rare occasions in my life when fear made me do the right thing.

In the meantime another German girl, Marrianne, arrived from my home town. We knew each other from our schooldays. She quickly hated Clarendon as I did.

As soon as I had entered the school I had been unhappy in the top section of the house. By now I was frightened of being alone. In my room the evil presence flitted about whenever I was by myself, and what few objects there were sometimes had minds of their own. The door would often fly

open to frighten me. Even with the window closed and a
small electric fire pumping out heat I was frozen – but not
with ordinary cold. This was a cold that chilled me inside.

I smoked more than ever and began to drink more. When I
could get to the village I would buy any sort of pills I could
afford. Things were getting out of hand.

It wasn't long before I was called before Matron, a kindly
Christian who was fair but firm. I was threatened: 'If you
don't stop, Gabriele, you will be sent home.'

The other girls had prophesied the threat. 'But she won't
send you home,' one told me. 'They can't get anyone to work
here except us.'

My rebellion extended beyond solitary drinking. I decided
to celebrate my twentieth birthday in style with my friends. I
'borrowed' a bowl and poured into it everything I could get;
fruit juice, wine, cognac, and any other ingredients that were
likely to add to its potency. That evening I invited the others
to my room. We drank every drop. I was ill for three days.
But even that was a sort of revenge on their authority – I
couldn't work.

I also got my own back by stealing drugs from the
medicine cupboard as soon as I discovered where the key
was kept. The sleeping tablets I took could not however
drive away the nightly apparitions which haunted me.

During the Second World War Kinmel – the old name for
the school – had been taken over as a military hospital and in
October 1944 a fatal operation had taken place there. I
wondered if it had been in the area of my room. Whatever
the reason I was becoming more and more afraid and,
because I did not believe the other staff would understand, it
was a burden I bore alone. The fact was that I felt an evil
presence in the part of the building in which I lived, but no-
one else did. Six years after I left, that section was burnt
in a fire which gutted the building. The fire had started
in the area of my room... and when a Christian group
re-opened the hall that particular section was not opened.

Anyway, to bring some fun into my boring existence I
decided to have a holiday in Scotland. I booked in at a
Liverpool travel agent's for a 'Twilight Tour' of Scotland. It

looked just right. I paid my money and dreamed of late-night discos and all-night fun. When I boarded the coach I discovered what 'Twilight' meant – elderly! I was the only traveller under sixty. The pensioners spoiled me and I allowed them to do so – it was the only way to get some benefit from my mistake.

Back in Clarendon I continued to find the working conditions difficult. Then, one evening my friends and I heard scuffling noises in the garden near the washing lines.

The next morning we discovered all our washing in the swimming pool at the back of the school.

At first I laughed. It looked a funny sight, all our clothes, underwear and all, floating in the pool. Even the hours I had spent washing them didn't seem to matter. Then I saw Matron and heard her explain that no-one would be allowed to swim out to collect the washing – 'It is, after all, a Sunday!'

Then she realised I was watching and because I wasn't a Christian reckoned it was in order for me to change into my costume, swim out and collect the clothes. But even then we weren't allowed to dry them or even re-hang them on the line. That was work. It all seemed so petty that I determined to leave.

That evening Marrianne and I sat on my bed plotting. She had had enough as well. We decided to go to Ireland, and quickly.

We collected our suitcases from the attic and started to pack.

The next day we had an afternoon off. Marrianne had switched her free time to coincide with mine. We ordered a taxi and waited. When the taxi arrived we threw everything in, in total rebellion, not caring a bit about anyone or anything.

'The station at Prestatyn,' we said.

As we edged between the entrance pillars and shuddered over the cattle-grid I didn't even bother to look back. Clarendon School was behind me. That was where it was going to stay.

At the station we directed our suitcases to Victoria in

London – and bought tickets to Holyhead. From there we sailed to Ireland for a week or so before flying to the Isle of Man and returning to Liverpool. It was a carefree life ... just the two of us and our dwindling reserves of money.

It was about three months before Marrianne and I finally reached London together and collected our luggage, amazed that it had arrived at its destination and was still there!

Having our luggage was one thing; having somewhere to take it was another. My drug-filled mind recalled that one of the ladies on the staff at Clarendon had promised to get in touch with someone 'nice' on our behalf, in the hope of getting us work. It was a Christian place, of course: London Bible College. God's hand was surely in my remembering this, and in our telephoning from the station to find out if there might be a place for us. There was! Considering all that had gone before, it was amazing the staff were willing to take us on.

5

A NEW LIFE

Scratching together the remains of our money we called a taxi.

We had just enough money to get there with a little to spare, and we leaned thankfully back in the black interior, thinking how lucky we were. I had only taken the address and phone number of the college to avoid offending the lady at Clarendon.

We stopped outside an imposing building – newer in appearance than many in the area. We paid the driver, grabbed armfuls of cases and struggled through the glass doors.

The smell of food came from the left as we entered – the dining room, I discovered later. I spoke through a glass window to a girl at the reception desk. She clicked away on the internal telephone and a few minutes later a woman came to greet us. She showed us to our accommodation but as this meant grabbing the suitcases and going back out of the building, she asked a couple of students if they would help. The two young men took a couple of cases each and led the way back out through the glass doors. We followed the dull yellow-painted brickwork round to the left and turned into a side road – Nottingham Place. Huge buildings towered above me and a first-floor balcony seemed to run the length of the street, an iron railing guarding the edge. On my left were more railings, protecting pedestrians from a steep drop into the area outside basement flats. It was down there Marrianne and I were taken. The small room I was shown to actually looked out – if that can conceivably be the right expression – on to the area. I peered upwards and could make out the iron railings. They gave the room a prison-like appearance. It was not something that worried me, however. After three months of living rough, chasing from hostel to hostel, the thought of being in the same place for any length of time was in itself appealing.

Our work was simple: prepare meals for the hundred and fifty students and staff, clean the rooms – including the students' flats, the toilets, endless corridors and stairs – and ward off the enthusiastic young Christians who plied us with literature and 'spiritual advice for the good of our souls'.

My soul wasn't doing too badly, I considered. I managed without the advice. Except for one student who somehow seemed more understanding – and certainly less pushy – than his colleagues: Peter Holmes. I was working in the stainless steel atmosphere of the kitchen when I met Peter. Elbow-deep in slimy, foam-covered washing-up water, I was scrubbing away at the interiors of an apparently endless row of huge cooking pots when he wandered into the kitchen.

He stood alongside me and said: 'You're German.'

I thought: 'What a stupid thing to say.'

I discovered later he was noticing the lines on my face and decided I needed help. He sensed in that first meeting that I was on drugs. I don't know how . . . no-one else had noticed or appeared to care at home, school or even in the college. Drumming religion into me was one thing . . . being interested seemed somehow different.

Work at the college was tough and the office staff and full-time lecturers were boring Christians in my eyes, but the small group of au pairs were out most evenings touring the London sights, or spending what little they could afford in different entertainment places.

The only real friend I had during this period was Marrianne and we spent our evenings drinking or smoking, sometimes going out if we could afford it. Smoking was awkward, for we had to do it outside the house, surreptitiously – it was strictly forbidden within the college buildings.

I had conflicting problems: I couldn't bear to be alone because the visions and noises were as frequent as ever and just as nerve-racking in the Christian environment as they had been in the past; but at the same time my increasingly depressed state made me want to withdraw from other people. I became more of a loner, preferring my own company to that of the other girls.

With my mind dulled from drugs I would puzzle over what lay in store – afraid of the future. My parents' words, 'You'll be back', kept coming to mind; life as an au pair was not worthwhile but was I capable of anything better?

Drugs were easy to come by. A small chemist's shop in nearby Marylebone High Street sold a selection of tablets and I was a good customer. Often, to hide the amount I was taking. I would visit other chemists – the all-night one at Piccadilly being a favourite haunt. It was handy for other reasons; stronger drugs could be bought from the characters who frequented the area, congregating round the base of Eros like market traders. A friend in Asper even sent me valium by post.

Life had its lighter moments although they too were tinged with doom. From my worm's-eye view of the world I often saw the students drifting by – they lived in accommodation blocks alongside ours. They wore long black gowns and as they swept by the corner of the building, the wind tugging at their tails, they looked for all the world like a succession of bats circling over an unlucky mouse.

And often I would witness their idiotic pranks. I had just finished in the kitchen one morning when I saw a strange group making their way across the main road towards Regent's Park. Half-a-dozen students had lashed another unfortunate student in his bed – still in his pyjamas – and were carrying him, iron bed and all. I learnt later from Peter that they made directly for a shallow lake and dropped him in – bed included.

The soaking student had to struggle free and drip his way back to college. I never did find out how he got the bed back . . . or, indeed, if he did.

Just being able to laugh reminded me that there must be fun in the world. Later that day as I lay with my mind dulled by pills I could not prevent my imagination from exploring some of the suggestions Peter had made. 'Give God a chance,' he said once. It was tempting... but then a shadowy vision drifted across the room, and I knew it would never work. Whatever it was that had me in its grip it would never release me. I was doomed to be bound for the rest of my life.

Fortunately Peter didn't share my feelings of failure.

With pop star Cliff Richard singing and talking at Kensington Temple (a London church), on a Sunday evening at the end of November – two months after I had begun work at the college – I was easy prey for the invitation.

I had watched Cliff Richard and The Shadows just a week before, at the London Palladium, and loved every minute of it; one of my rare nights out at that time. So on Sunday, Peter and I and a group of other students processed down the escalator at Baker Street Underground station for the short journey to Notting Hill Gate.

When we finally stood outside the church it looked like everything I hated... pointed, stained-glass windows, and heavy wooden doors. Inside it was just as forbidding – rows of wooden pews, and a balcony that twisted round three sides of the building, pointing towards a platform.

I decided I wasn't going to enjoy it. The initial singing might have been lively but I hardly uttered a sound. Then Cliff sang and still I felt nothing. It just didn't impress me. 'So this is Cliff Richard, the Christian...' I thought.

But when he started to talk, although I had only been in Britain for eight months and still had problems with the language, somehow I could understand every word. As he spoke light seemed to flicker its way into my darkened mind. It was as if someone were opening curtains that had been drawn for years and allowing the sun to shine.

'For God so loved the world that he gave his one and only Son, that whoever believes in him shall not perish but have eternal life,' Cliff was pointing out, telling us the verse came from John's Gospel, chapter 3 v 16. Jesus left heaven, became man, and died for us, he went on. 'He died to save you from your sins. Just ask him to forgive you and allow him to live through you.' I was held by every word.

Even I knew what he meant when he asked anyone

wanting Jesus in their lives to go forward to the front of the church – and I went. I don't know how I made it, but I found myself at the platform forgetting everyone and everything. I stood with a dozen or so other people and repeated the prayer Cliff recited. The curtains twitched open another fraction; more light shone.

I was taken into a small room, behind the platform somewhere, and a couple of women talked and prayed with me, and I began to realise it wasn't going to be as simple as they thought. 'Pray and read your Bible,' they coaxed, giving me a small card to fill in and some other literature which they assured me would be helpful. I tried to explain about the drugs, the drinking and the dark shadowy images I sensed when alone. 'I am frightened by them,' I explained.

'Just pray, dear,' one of the women told me. 'It will be all right – God won't fail you.'

It seemed simple. I longed to believe her. Deep down I wasn't so sure.

Even as they prayed I sensed the curtains closing . . . I cried and stretched out to keep them open but failed. The women were unimpressed by my fear of demons. 'Jesus is the answer,' they kept saying.

Reluctantly I bowed my head. 'Ah well,' I prayed. 'If you are real, Jesus, here is my life. You can have it. And if you are real, please show me. If you want me to follow you, give me an exciting life . . .'

One of the women peeped at me. Perhaps it was an unusual prayer – I could see surprise in her eyes.

But God was to fulfil both requests: I would discover he was alive – and I would find excitement. Perhaps too much!

As I slipped into bed that evening it was with the hope that things would be different. They were. Horribly so.

The other girls in the flat were away so I was alone. As I tried to sleep I heard a noise. Footprints stamped into the room. I sensed a figure materialising in front of me. My eyes opened and I screamed. In front of me stood a demon, not a shadowy shape, but reality and certainty, not a figment of my imagination or fear. The demon moved and suddenly reappeared in another part of the room. Fear gripped me. I felt myself freezing inside as if an ice-making machine had suddenly begun to solidify my body.

On the floor our pet cat was sitting howling, absolutely terrified, waving her paws at the demon – and weaving about in an effort to fend off the evil that was scaring us both. I started to scream again and collapsed...

When I came to, different people were helping me. Peter arrived, I don't know how he knew, and tried to calm me. A raw recruit who didn't know what deliverance was, he prayed. Even with his inexperience of the occult he had realised that if I were deeper in Christ I would have extra protection. I prayed with him, fervently now, realising that this was going to be a battle I had to win. Since I was little I had been frightened by the constant visions and noises but had been told it was my overworked imagination. I had been unable to believe that and now I was discovering it was definitely not that simple. There was something evil – and it was always lurking in my vicinity. I needed more power, and I felt weak and unable to fight.

Following my decision in church that Sunday I began to pray and read my Bible. The principal of the college, Gilbert Kirby – a gentle and lovely man – even allowed me to attend some lectures when my working timetable allowed. And I felt myself starting to grow in the things of God.

At Kensington Temple I began to enjoy the meetings, particularly the preaching of Eldin Corsie, the minister, who was also very helpful to me. He certainly didn't seem to despise my fears of the devil, and because of his influence I decided to be baptised. My Bible knowledge was very limited but I realised that Jesus had been baptised and considered that a good enough recommendation. I prayed and talked with Mr Corsie on a few occasions before the ceremony and discovered that I would have to give a testimony at the time I was baptised.

I didn't know what a testimony was until Peter explained that it was just a short talk about how I had become a Christian. The prospect scared me. My English was not very good and I had a lifetime of shyness behind me. I just could

not imagine standing in front of people and talking.
Fortunately Mr Corsie was understanding. 'Write it down
and read it,' he suggested. It seemed the perfect answer.

So just a couple of months after my conversion I was to
be baptised. But on the Thursday before the Sunday service I
suddenly felt ill, with sickness and pains in my head. It
seemed that everything was conspiring against me. Ironically
it was also my day off. It seemed a waste. I decided to spend
the day in my room without eating, reading my Bible and
praying. I only discovered afterwards about fasting, so
perhaps God was introducing me to spiritual principles early
on in my young Christian life.

Whatever it was I felt stronger for it. When I arrived for
the baptism the church seemed very different from how it
had on my first visit. I felt at home and looked with longing
at the water in the sunken baptismal pool at the front of the
church. I was taken to a back room and dressed in a long
white gown (weighted in the hem to prevent it floating), and
then sat at the front of the packed church.

Despite my usual nervousness and inexperience at doing
anything in front of others I felt God's hands lifting me up
and giving me an extraordinary confidence. As I faced the
people and was introduced, I heard Pastor Corsie say:
'Gabriele has a word of testimony.'

My eyes clouded over and I couldn't read the paper with
my carefully prepared script, but words began to come. An
incredible peace soaked into me and I stood, almost listening
to myself speak – it was as if someone else were talking for
me.

And then I entered the pool. I hardly heard the words 'in
the name of the Father, Son and Holy Spirit' when I drifted
backwards under the warm water, sensing as I did so the
absolute goodness of God and the wonder of Jesus' love for
me. I rose a new person anxious to face a new life.

A promise was given to me that day: 'The Lord is good, a
stronghold in the day of trouble, and he knoweth them that
trust in him' (Nahum 1:7, AV).

As I received the congratulations of my friends, other
students and the folk of the church I felt near to heaven. It

was bliss. Surely nothing could harm me now.

But I had reckoned without Satan. The Evil One had been given charge of my life at six months and refused to give me up.

I was on cloud nine for just one week before things collapsed. It happened as it had on so many other occasions when I was alone in my room. Once again it was the weird, horrifying demon that brought the frighteningly rude awakening. Yes, I was saved by Jesus – but Satan had not given up on me. I had entered a new life, but there was still too much of the old within me which wasn't dealt with yet.

Drifting round the room he petrified me. But as suddenly as he came he disappeared and I fled from the room. I hurtled out of the building knocking over a small table in my desperate flight. I didn't know where I was going nor did I care. Eventually I ended up in Piccadilly Circus and within minutes had bought enough drugs to knock me out and blot out the horrible vision that taunted me.

It was only a day or so before I was once more hooked on drugs and my newly-won freedom had been lost.

Was I still a Christian? Did Christ still love me? Peter tried to tell me he did. I couldn't agree. Failure hits hard. And if God was all-powerful why didn't he protect me from these demonic attacks? Surely that wasn't too much for a young Christian to ask?

As the drugs took effect my mind told me that only death could end the torment. I waited until the other girls were out one evening and then went into the bathroom taking a pair of old scissors, the only thing I could find capable of cutting.

I sat on the edge of the bath, leaning over the hand basin and slashed at my wrists – this time I didn't want to repeat the childish failure of my attempt many years before in my father's study.

I didn't fail. As I cut I watched the blood spurt out, clouding the water in the basin into an instant vat of red. I sank to the floor, waiting to drift into the end of life. But as I waited I realised my hands were turning white. As they took on their frightening new appearance I watched the cut marks on my wrist . . . the blood stopped pumping out . . . the cuts began to close up and smooth over. I leapt from the floor in a new agony of terror.

What was happening to me? I couldn't live – and I couldn't die. Something demonic had bound me to sickness, pain and Satan; now I sensed I was also bound to another force, unable even to halt my life.

For the second time in as many months I was taken to the sick-bay. Peter sat for hours at my bed-side talking, praying, reading the Bible, or simply saying nothing... just being there.

A nurse was always in attendance and all the sharp objects were noticeably out of reach. When Peter wasn't around a tape-recorder droned out a constant diet of scripture songs or Bible readings which seemed to keep me calm.

Once back at work I discovered an appointment had been made for me to see Arthur Wallis who might be able to help me. He lived in South London and had some experience in dealing with the occult, I was told. In a telephone conversation he agreed to see me and promised to fast and pray for me.

One of the female members of staff at LBC took me down by train to keep the appointment. The nearer we got the more fidgety I became, twisting around in the seat – and the more frightened I was. Something told me it was a turning point; but something else also kept telling me it was a waste of time.

As soon as Arthur opened the door of his home I was gripped with fear. I knew he understood. For the first time in my life I felt someone actually knew what I was going through. I shook as he led me into his room. With a gentle kindness he began to talk and pray. As he did so I realised he was telling me things from my past that he could not possibly have found out. How did he know? I was more frightened than ever. But my fear of his stream of revelations was overcome by the knowledge that if I left his house without his help it would be at the cost of abandoning the Christian life which I had begun to sense was the answer to all my problems.

The voices in my head persisted: 'You'll never make it. You don't belong here...'

Arthur continued to pray. He focussed specifically on my past, reconstructing it with no help from me. Then he renounced it on my behalf and prayed to cut me off from it. He asked Jesus to protect me against drugs – and as he did so I felt something leave me. I could not explain it afterwards when Peter asked me what happened. I just sensed something leaving me – something evil. It was a horrible feeling, yet it brought relief.

As he continued to talk Arthur closed the curtains to screen the rain that was beating outside, and my fears heightened. Only his charming personality and the warmth and sincerity of his prayers got me through the afternoon. Eventually, drained and weak, I leaned back in the armchair on the edge of which I had been precariously perched.

He looked into my eyes and spoke gently. 'We have demanded that the craving for drugs will leave you – I believe it has. We have prayed that you will be delivered from the past – I believe it will come. It will, however, be a long, hard battle. You must view it as a battle and call upon Jesus continually.'

His warning couldn't have been more accurate. It was to be another couple of months before the hold drugs had on me was beaten: it would be many years before I would find freedom from the other influences on my life.

After my visit to Arthur Wallis I thought more about the past and tried to piece together the missing elements of my life. It was difficult. But somewhere in the back of my mind I knew that there were influences trying to harm me; influences that had suddenly roared into offensive action at my conversion. But how could I fight them?

It was Peter who gave me the clue. 'Just tell the demon you have been saved and are kept by the blood of Jesus Christ... Tell him he can't harm you.'

Ironically it was some of the other domestic helpers at the London Bible College who helped me test his words. One or two workers were on drugs and one woman was deeply involved in the occult; unfortunately she lived in the same flat as myself. I had rejected invitations to attend seances but I couldn't escape her influence, realising, for instance, that outside my window was a metal grille and painted on it was an occult sign – a call sign locking the area into a demonic network.

On one occasions she came to my room and tried to involve me in her wicked games. I repeated the prayer Peter had suggested and she ran barefoot out of the building and didn't come back to me.

If that made me over-confident my birthday brought me down to earth just a couple of days later.

It was March the second – my twenty-first birthday – and I had a free day. As I sat in my room a church bell rang out – a quarter past eleven in the morning. The door opened with a squeaking sound – the demon was back. This time, however, it was not the same figure I had experienced before but instantly I knew who was behind it – my aunt. The aunt who had sold me to Satan as a baby. She was back to watch over her charge.

As I stared open-mouthed at the frightening apparition, the demon laughed ... a horrible, chilling laugh. It was the answer to my twenty-one year struggle with evil. As the fact sank into my mind I drifted into a faint. Because I didn't leave my room Peter came down and invited me out for the rest of the day to cheer me up. He took me to meet Reuben, a pastor from Nigeria who was living in London while studying for a Master's degree in Theology. He too was willing to help in my struggle and to wait patiently for God to work.

The next day a letter arrived from my mother and I was not surprised to see the airline ticket. Her pleading stirred something inside me. Perhaps it would be better to go home and be the person I was destined to be from a child. Peter and Reuben couldn't prevent me. Weighed under with advice I took my small holdall, looked back at the college which had been my home for six months, and stepped into a taxi that would take me to London's Heathrow Airport. The letter had been the final straw. Depressed because I seemed unable to achieve the victory my new faith appeared to promise, I was too weak to live like a Christian. I was convinced that in Germany life would be easier – I would have a job and money, and escape the stress brought on by Christianity.

Almost mechanically I moved from the taxi through the reception area and boarded my flight.

Perhaps God wasn't all they cracked him up to be. Perhaps there was a stronger force in the world. In Germany we would see!

6

FINDING FRIENDS

It was Easter when I flew home. In a daze I walked off the plane and through the customs desk in Stuttgart Airport. Father and mother were waiting for me. Mother was all over me, hugging and kissing me and sobbing. Father just patted my hand and moved away. I left them for a few minutes and returned to the customs hall to claim my suitcase – Stuttgart is an unusual airport for the lay-out allows passengers to mingle with non-passengers before collecting their luggage.

As I returned with my case my father didn't speak but took the suitcase and tipped it into the boot of his car parked near the entrance. I sat in the back of the car; my mother was still sobbing quietly. No-one spoke as we drove home.

For days my father refused to speak. When I was in bed I could hear him shouting and arguing with mother. 'She will never make it.'

Mother spent the days blackmailing me. 'My nice little daughter doesn't exist any more. How can you treat us like this after all we've done. Why don't you stay at home and let me look after you?'

The silence from father and whining from mother twisted my nerves tighter. I flitted from chemist's to chemist's to get drugs. Normal conversation was impossible. I realised I was drifting away from all reality. In some ways my father was right. I was a worthless failure.

One glimmer of hope came late one evening. I met Manfred again – the young man from the Methodist church whom I had liked so much. I told him frankly what had happened to me, and what was happening. He was polite and nice and talked until two o'clock in the morning but couldn't help. It seemed the last straw. My resistance finally cracked.

As I walked the darkened streets of Asperg on my way home the darkness matched my life. Again suicide appeared the only way out. This time with no mistakes. The depression and pills had robbed me of any will to live.

I crept into the flat taking care not to wake my parents. The last thing I wanted now was a scene. When they found the body then they could mourn, although it didn't matter to me. In my mind I believed they were more interested in their own egos than my future. I guessed they would be angry that I had brought yet another slur on the family name. In a way it would be an appropriate revenge – taking my life in their flat. After all that was where my life had never been allowed to develop.

But after I had gently opened the door the dim light from the hall revealed a letter addressed to me on the table, not just addressed but smothered in stamps, express and registered. I grabbed a kitchen knife from the drawer and slit the envelope open. Slowly I withdrew the contents – sensing as I did so what they would be and who they would be from. It was a one-way ticket, Stuttgart-to-London, with a short note. 'Accommodation is provided. Take the next plane and come. Love, Peter.'

My numb mind at least knew I had to act immediately. The next morning I telephoned Lufthansa and booked a flight for later the same day. Then I crept into my bedroom and began to re-pack the suitcase that had only spilled its contents over the room a few days earlier. By the time my parents were awake I was ready to leave.

'I'm leaving,' I said.

Either there must have been something so certain in my voice that any response was useless, of it was beyond their comprehension. They didn't answer. They were still shocked when they took me to the airport. I marched through the customs hall without even looking back, leaving behind a weeping mother and frustrated father. I wished I could cry... but I felt like a stone.

This time I wouldn't return. I didn't want to see my parents again. On the plane I felt sick and scared. I fumbled in my handbag and shovelled out a handful of pills. Taking a little plastic cup and filling it with the contents of the small miniature bottle of Scotch the stewardess delivered to me I stuffed the pills into my mouth and swallowed the drink. I remember nothing else about the hour or so's flight. All I recall is aiming my gradually more disobedient body towards one of the electric doors at Heathrow Airport, watching the doors swish apart, and falling through them into Peter's arms. Only through prayer did he know which door I would pass through, just as prayer had told him, and some of his friends, that I was in deadly trouble in Asperg and had led to his sending the ticket.

Into the rear of his blue and white car went the suitcase and I sprawled out in the front seat.

As he drove he talked, his words drifting in and out of my mind. I realised that we were now parked alongside the Thames, and as his voice droned on I watched the waters flow past, broken by little waves and the occasional chunk of driftwood. That's how I felt, drifting along with circum-stances forcing me to go their way.

Peter realised I was not paying attention. He snapped at me and the change in his voice made me look. 'Listen to me,' he stormed. 'You have to make up your mind. Either you want to come off those drugs or you don't. If you do, throw them all in the river. We'll take care of you. I have a couple of friends who have promised to help you. You can live with them. But I'm only interested if you want to make the effort... it's your decision.'

With that he leaned back in his seat, obviously praying. I thought he looked obstinate. But he was right, I knew he was right. If I meant business I had to start somewhere.

For two hours I battered him with words, suddenly coming to life. Ignoring everything I said he sat implacable, just occasionally reminding me of his promise. 'Throw them away and we'll take care of you.'

Eventually I knew what I had to do. I flung myself out of the car, slammed the door behind me and stumbled towards the bank of the Thames. My bag was in my hand and I dragged the contents out, spilling them across the grass in front of me. Scuffling on the ground I picked out the pills, turning to Peter with a wave of triumph, and threw them into the water. I stood and watched them disappear with a great desire to jump after them.

I slipped the rest of the contents of my bag back inside it and yanked the door of the car open. 'Satisfied?' I said in a weak voice. I leaned inside and pushed myself into the seat.

Peter didn't speak; he merely turned on the engine, let out the clutch and twisted the wheel to direct us back on to the road.

I was taken to a semi-detached house in Wimbledon. We went up a small drive beside a neat garden and pressed the doorbell. A sweet old lady answered the ring and ushered us inside where another lady also greeted us. Mrs Bray and Mrs Hitchcock were to look after me for some time. We sat and drank tea from china cups, a small plate of biscuits in the very centre of the table. And then I was shown to my room. In seconds I was asleep, and for once my mind switched off. I was allowed to lose myself in the blissful rest that only deep sleep can bring... until about six o'clock in the morning. A rattling, knocking noise roused me and immediately I was treated to a range of my usual demonic visitations. I was petrified but afraid to impose my fears on the old ladies, so I waited until I heard them moving about downstairs a couple of hours later before daring to slip on my dressing-gown and leave the bedroom.

'Good morning, God bless you,' were the words that greeted my arrival. But neither of the ladies had spoken; the words came from a colourful parrot perched in a cage in a corner of the room. His cheerful Christian greeting would later make me smile every time I heard it. On that first morning, however, it was just another odd experience to add to my others.

The ladies were at work; one busy dusting in one room, the other sitting with a Bible in her hand praying. That was their calling, they told me: one worked – the other prayed. They took turns.

When Peter called later that morning my frustrations bubbled to the surface as I recounted my early morning experiences.

'I can't understand it,' he said. 'This is a clean house – demon-free. No-one knew you were here.'

On an intuition he ordered me into his car and I obeyed.

He flung the car into street after street as if demons were after us. It was like being in a police chase. I gasped a question – 'What are you doing?' – but all I could gather was that he had decided that my family had a demonic hold over me. He believed they had the power to identify where I was at any given moment and the hair-raising drive was to give them the slip.

It was a manoeuvre he was to repeat and amazingly it seemed to work, for I always had peace for a few days afterwards as if it took the evil guardians time to track me down again.

Peter did not live too far from the old ladies in Wimbledon. I had first been to his little terraced house when he was celebrating his twenty-first birthday some months before. His parents had a deep faith and a quiet confidence that was being passed on to their son. They had been extremely kind to me and a month or so after I had moved into the area they invited me to live with them, sharing a room with two of Peter's sisters – loving girls who were a few years younger than me.

On one occasion I was talking to Bob – Peter's father – when he asked an unusual question. 'Why do you always wear trousers?' he said, looking at my suit.

It was such an odd question I laughed. 'Because they are all I have.'

I thought the subject was finished until it was time to go to bed when Bob pressed something into my hand and squeezed my fingers round it. 'Buy yourself a dress, Gaby,' he told me.

It was such a touching act from a family with little money to spare. At first I visualised myself in something from the latest Dior collection . . . but within a day or two the money had been put to a more sinister use: I bought drugs. That evening when Peter saw me I had to confess. Guilt burned inside me. But it was only one of many emotions – I was also riddled with self-pity and feared the reaction of his father. Peter assured me his father still loved me. I wasn't so certain, afraid of losing my newly gained home.

When I saw Bob it was as if it had never happened. No-one mentioned my misuse of the money. Bob put his arms round me and kissed me. A second time he took my hand and put something in it: the same amount of money as before. He smiled and led me to the table for the evening meal. I was perplexed and hardly knew how to react. Could he really love me so much? Never before had I experienced a father's love like that.

The warm feeling lasted precisely five days. Then hopelessness hit me again. I left the peace of the Wimbledon home and made my way to Piccadilly Circus, buying more drugs from the all-night chemist. I must have taken too many; I collapsed in the underground station and was taken to a nearby hospital.

When the doctor asked me what was wrong I lied. I told him I had gall-bladder problems, pointing out that I had had an operation some years before. The scar on my stomach confirmed the story. To my joy and surprise they injected me with morphine against the pain. The morphine on top of the other drugs I had taken proved too much for my system and I went wildly on a horror trip.

It took only seconds for the doctors to realise that I had lied and that I was a drug addict. My room was changed and I found myself in a windowless, single room with no door handle on the inside. My clothes were taken away and the door shut.

Now the pain hit me. My head was in agony. I reeled with the intensity of it. And the faces appeared; demonic grinning faces that flashed all round me, tormenting and taunting. All night the torment went on, leaving me helpless and shivering.

Next morning I was asked for a name for the hospital authorities to contact. I gave them Peter's name and the Bible College address. An hour or two later he came to collect me. I never knew how I managed to leave the hospital. Peter told me afterwards many students at the college had prayed and he himself had assured the hospital authorities he would take care of me.

I was returned to Peter's family. They were love itself. Hour after hour Bob sat and talked, his quiet voice soothing away the pains. It was therapeutic, but still I felt cold, as like a stone inside unable to laugh or cry.

I managed to keep off drugs for some time. It seemed, however, as if something was blocking my access to God. I couldn't approach him. My prayers seemed to rebound off the ceiling and Jesus seemed to be miles away.

Suicide again seemed the only answer. It was a Saturday evening and Peter was home for the weekend when the attack started. I began to shiver and shake. Peter pushed away the Bible he was reading and the sermon notes he was preparing and told me to hold his hand. I couldn't. Inside I was still frozen, unable to touch and unwilling to be touched, especially by a man.

Peter didn't move. He stayed beside me on the sofa just radiating love and patience. Time didn't matter to him. We sat until five o'clock in the morning, Peter implacably praying and loving; I resisting and rejecting any thought of God.

Then Peter acted. He went to the bathroom and returned with a pack of new razor blades. He put the pack into my hand and told me to go into the garden. 'Kill yourself. I can't stop you any more.'

Silently I left the room. As I opened the back door and stepped into the garden the darkness swallowed me up. It was as if I was made for darkness. A sadistic joy inside me surged up. 'I've got you now,' I heard an inward voice say.

I unwrapped one of the blades and, as the paper cover dropped away, pressed the edge against my wrist. For the fourth time in my life I was only seconds from death. The blackness became denser. I was about to push the blade home when Peter's arm slid round my back. He gently took the blades and half carried me back into the house.

Suddenly the stone cracked. Like a dam that had burst I

began to cry. The tears that had refused to come for so long now poured out like a torrent.

As I wept Peter's mother pushed the door open from the stairs. She looked inside, realised it was me making the noise that had obviously disturbed her, pulled the door shut and went back to bed. With sensitivity and reticence she never mentioned the incident.

All the time I cried Peter held me in his arms, like a big brother, a father, a minister and counsellor rolled into one.

When the tears finally stopped it was nine o'clock in the morning. Two hours later Peter was to preach in a Baptist church. Because of me he had no sermon and no time to prepare. But he didn't seem bothered, he was too full of joy. He sensed, as I did, a breakthrough that was going to begin to rebuild my life.

He took me to church with him, sat me in a back seat and told me to pray. 'Pray that God will give me a sermon,' he asked. I did.

Peter preached a fine sermon. People were obviously moved. Then he called me to the front of the church. Shaking I went. 'A testimony older than a day is history,' he told the congregation. 'Gabriele, tell the folk here what God has done for you today.'

It seemed a mean, underhand trick, but it worked. For five minutes the Lord carried me, somehow helping me to explain the complex work that had begun in me in the early hours of the morning.

As I walked back to my seat I reflected: it was my first testimony since my baptism five months before. At last I had done something for Jesus. I had ministered to people.

Peter and his family sat round their cosy little room later that evening as I stumbled through another testimony. I told them how grateful I was to them for their love and care. 'How can I ever give you back what you have given me? All the time, money, love... how?' I asked.

There was silence. Peter spoke. 'By doing just the same for those who will come to you for help.' Bob and his wife smiled at the wisdom displayed by their son and nodded.

And deep down I knew that in this lay the answer not just to my question – but to my life.

7

MIRACLES

A beaming sun grinned down from a blue sky. The grass was green and seemed to stretch for miles. And on one side a quaint windmill poked its sails above the trees as if reaching for the sun. Peter, Reuben and I were walking on Wimbledon Common enjoying the July weather. I had been off drugs for three months, their joint counselling had given me a strength I hadn't thought possible and my life was beginning to lose the traumatic edge that had marked it.

As we sat Reuben pointed to a huge oak tree spreading its enormous branches over us. 'Look at its strength. Its roots go deep into the earth drawing life, and its branches stretch upwards – towards heaven – to take the benefits of the light. That's how you are beginning to grow,' he told me.

Peter nodded his approval. 'So long as you feed on God's word and make sure your foundations are in that word you will grow strong,' Peter pointed out – an apt metaphor.

'And make sure you stretch upwards, always looking to God for light, guidance, help,' Reuben added.

Gently they then brought up the reason for the walk and talk. Peter took up the conversation. 'We think you should go back to Germany to your family and live your Christian life there. Make your family your first mission field. When they have come to the Lord, you will be released to serve Jesus wherever he leads you.' My mind was trying to grasp the shock of the thought of returning home. It would be, I felt, to court disaster. I remembered the depression and the drugs that had tempted me when I was there before. I couldn't take it.

Unfortunately even as I was making my excuses I was

hearing a voice inside me confirming their convictions. Peter related the story of the Philippian jailor from Acts 16, and told me again that, like the jailor, when my family had become Christian, I would be freed to reach others, words that were to become true after much pain... In the open air, with the rest of the world concentrating on the tennis that was taking place just a mile or so away – the Lawn Tennis Championships – I felt the weight of the world on my shoulders.

As they both prayed the shock began to leave me, and the fears were replaced by a confidence that perhaps it could work; perhaps I could return home and God would be strong enough to keep me from the dangers of drugs and depression.

A few weeks later – in August – I packed a suitcase and Peter drove me once again in his little car; this time towards London Airport. As we purred steadily along the three-lane road and turned off into the airport complex, dipping under an underpass and then swinging round towards the terminal, I began to question the advisability of my decision. Mother was in a sanatorium because she had suffered a breakdown and father of course had hardly spoken a reasonable word to me for years. For two hours I sobbed... it was fortunate we had that much time to spare.

Peter provided the supply of dry handkerchiefs and also a prophetic word I knew was from God. 'You will be very much in the arms of the Lord and stay in his love and peace.' The prophecy, he explained, would be needed as soon as I returned home. He was convinced I would find the situation so hard there that only God's love could cope.

Throughout the flight I was praying, calling on God to give me the strength I was going to need. I knew I was in his will; I knew his mighty hand was holding me up.

God demonstrated his concern as soon as I arrived at Stuttgart. My father was there to meet me. The journey home was made in silence. I didn't know what to say. I continued to ask God to tell me.

I put my suitcase on the floor of the flat and sat for a few minutes trying to decide how to start a conversation. But I needn't have bothered. Father started to talk immediately, telling me about mother and how they wanted me home. He had hardly begun when the doorbell rang. I went to the door intent on getting rid of whoever it was as quickly as possible so that we could continue the conversation. It was Ursula, the girl whom I had first met on the railway station and who had subsequently encouraged me at her church. She stepped inside, kissed me and started to welcome me back to Germany. Suddenly I was thrust to one side; father stormed at her. 'Get out,' he shouted. 'And don't come back.'

As she turned and left, bewildered by his behaviour, he turned on me. 'You asked her to come, didn't you? You arranged it so that you could leave me as soon as you got home. You don't want me, do you?'

While I tried to explain that I had had no idea Ursula would come, he snatched my suitcase and flung it through the door... it crashed its way down the stairs. Then he grabbed my arm and forced me through the door. 'I don't want to see you again,' he screamed. As he pushed the door to I managed to stick my foot into the gap, straining at the door.

Father rushed back to the sitting room and sat down in the sofa, bitterness and anger written across every line of his face.

At that moment I felt such a surge of God's love that while my reflexes told me to leave the flat, my body moved over to father. I sat down next to him and put an arm round his shoulders. 'I know that you love me, and I love you, believe me. You don't want me to go. Let's start again and forget the doorbell ever rang.'

For the first time in my life I saw my father break down. He sobbed with great convulsive shrugs of his shoulders.

Between sobs he told me he had known all about the drugs I was taking over the years but hadn't known how to help me. 'I just kept my mouth shut. I didn't know what to do,' he cried.

The news shook me. The father who I believed had never loved me in his life had all along been so aware of me, but unable to help. I realised the awful dilemma he had been in;

knowing that if he said the wrong thing it would do more harm than good.

As our arms wrapped each other in warmth and tear-stained love I knew that a new relationship had started.

It was a few weeks before mother came back home and if I thought that the new relationship between my father and me would make things easier I was wrong. In fact it made them worse.

As we talked about the drugs and my new Christianity she couldn't understand the reality of either. She could not admit the possibility that her daughter might have become a drug addict, even though I was called the 'well-dressed addict' by friends. My difficulty over convincing her that my new life with Jesus Christ was real and exciting was simple compared with the other problem I determined to tell her about – my aunt and the occult influence which had robbed me of life.

Pouting her lips in anger, she told me to decide: 'It's either Jesus or me. Make up your mind.'

I loved my mother. But I loved Jesus more. With my mouth I told her that I loved her the most – and in my heart I gave Jesus the same message. The situation tore me apart. I felt I had let my Lord down.

It wasn't long before I began to look for work. I had no idea what to do; obviously it was inconceivable that I should try for a doctor's receptionist again. It was too much of a temptation with drugs being available and in any case I felt a real revulsion at giving injections and handing out pills now.

But I did enjoy flying. So I went to the office of Lufthansa to see if they had any jobs. It could, I reasoned, give me cheap flights to London so that I could keep in touch with my friends. I knew it was a miracle when the answer came back a day or two later . . . 'Yes'. I was given a ticket to fly to Hamburg for three days for more tests and it was a tense, nervous Gabriele who made that journey, lacking the confidence needed for an interview.

In fact there were a string of interviews. One was quite remarkable. I faced a panel of three airline officials – each probing different aspects of my life. 'What is your goal, your aim in life?' the good-looking man at the end of the desk asked me. As they paused, waiting for my answer, I jumped in with both feet. 'My aim is to love my Lord Jesus and follow him.' I watched for their reactions.

If I thought it was going to cost me the job I was mistaken. For an hour we talked about God and Jesus and what Christianity meant to me. My first testimony in Germany was over. I passed the four weeks of training, got the job, and flew to Frankfurt a few days later to collect my new uniform – a smart dark blue jacket and skirt, turquoise blouse and a dark blue pill-box hat that perched on my head in a comical fashion attached only by the golden needle shaped like a bird: the Lufthansa symbol. Blue shoes, handbag and a raincoat completed the outfit.

It wasn't long before I was behind the counter in the Lufthansa office in Stuttgart explaining to customers how they could travel the world with my airline. It was a marvellous life with the added bonus that occasionally I would be invited to travel to other countries accompanying little children travelling without their parents. My job was to look after them ... and it provided me with several free trips to London.

Life was full and my testimony was being sharpened by conversations with so many people. My colleagues and boss were left in no doubt as to my faith, and I was beginning to enter into the life of the little Methodist church I had once despised.

In my enthusiasm I did anything – even agreeing to preach and take Sunday services. My first sermon from the circular wooden pulpit in the Methodist church was about healing. Nervously I used plenty of notes, talked a lot about what God had done for others and for me, encouraging the congregation to trust God.

I was burning to tell people about Jesus. The top floor of the church building was converted into a coffee bar to attract teenagers. The furniture was stripped out and coloured blankets covered the floorboards with the occasional old mattress to break the monotony. Cushions and more mattresses were spread round the walls. The large room was

wallpapered in plain blue with red curtains adding a splash
of colour. At one end of the room was the bar – for soft
drinks only – smothered in silver paper to give it a more
authentic disco appearance.

I loved touring the streets armed only with a few gospel
leaflets and my Bible – a gift from Gerhard the present
youth-leader in the Methodist church – inviting the
youngsters to join us in the coffee bar. Often we would have a
music group to shatter the quiet atmosphere and leave us
headachy, but delighted that it meant more kids had been
prepared to come in and join us. Occasionally a guest
speaker would agree to come and we showed films and had
'live' music.

The coffee bar began to draw a regular clientele. At
twenty-three years old, a new Christian myself, I became like
a mother to many youngsters.

Ursula and Manfred occasionally visited us but preferred
the more orderly atmosphere of the youth club – a Bible
study group catering for church teenagers.

Only one thing in the church worried me: I could never
bring myself to sit in one pew. The pastor later told me an old
man who always sat there had committed suicide; another
hint to my subconscious that I had a strange, awful gift for
identifying evil.

There were fun-filled holidays as well, when I and a
handful of helpers would leave the church behind to take a
few dozen children into the Black Forest for a couple of
weeks in the summer. The boys would sleep in tents and the
girls spent the nights in the hay-loft of a cow shed, while cows
chewed hay and ambled placidly about underneath. We
cooked on an open fire, played games and had Bible talks. I
enjoyed myself just as much when I went back to the office in
Stuttgart. The air stewardesses would sit in the rest room
talking about their holidays. Miami, Disneyland, and
Mexico were the names they bandied about. 'Where did you
go, Gaby?' they asked.

'The Black Forest with seventy kids,' was my answer.

They thought I was mad. But it was an opportunity to talk
about God.

After the years I had spent messing up my life it was wonderful to feel I was doing something useful at work and in my free time. God was very real.

Not that I did everything he wanted. I was typing a letter for a senior member of staff on one occasion when I made a mistake without realising it. Given the letter back later I was asked to correct it. In the hustle of the day I forgot. When Karin, my boss, saw me later I knew she would ask whether I had corrected the letter. And a voice inside me said: 'Don't lie.' But I did. Immediately a curtain was drawn over my prayers and sleep. Three days later I asked Karin if she would come out for a coffee during our break. In a café near our office I confessed my lie and asked for forgiveness. Tears came to my eyes as I told her how it had affected my walk with God. It was her turn to be tearful now. She couldn't believe anyone could ask forgiveness for such a small thing.

God was indeed good. He was also good on another occasion which could have cost me my job.

I was to fly from Stuttgart to Frankfurt and had agreed to meet Reuben at Frankfurt to talk over some problems I had. In my handbag were about twenty airline tickets I had promised to leave at the Lufthansa desk at Stuttgart. In my enthusiasm to meet my old friend I hurtled through the airport, boarded my plane and completely forgot. Such was my excitement at seeing Reuben that even when we met in Frankfurt I didn't remember. We booked a couple of rooms in a hotel and Reuben began to listen to my difficulties. He was showing me scriptures and, although there were Gideon Bibles in English and German in the hotel, I felt more at home with my own, so I popped up to my room to get it. As I opened my bag to take out the Bible I saw the tickets. My heart lurched, I almost fainted. Knowing the timetable as I did I knew that the next plane to Stuttgart was due to leave in five minutes and there was no way I could ever reach the airport in time to give the tickets to the captain and ask him to pass them on.

Reuben, my help on so many occasions in the past, simply prayed. Urging me to 'be at peace', he prayed for a delay in the flight. We ran to the lift and pumped the buttons. It arrived quickly and in our eagerness to get out as the doors opened, we almost ended up in the hotel swimming pool. We had gone down a floor too many. Back into the lift we ran and as it opened on the ground floor we hurtled through the glass swing doors, calling a taxi at the same time. All my pleading with the taxi driver to drive as quickly as he could did not remove the traffic en route! It took half-an-hour to get to the airport. The plane should now have been half-way to Stuttgart.

. Still Reuben urged me on. I talked my way through the barriers at the airport and asked for a service bus to the plane. Strangely enough they agreed – something unheard of, when I talked to friends afterwards. I was the only passenger as the coach ground its way round the airport to where the plane was still standing with its steps down... nearly thirty-five minutes after it should have been airborne.

The crew told me the other strange fact. 'When we tried to start the engine nothing happened. We had clearance to begin to taxi to the runway but the engine just wouldn't start.'

I couldn't believe what was happening. I handed the tickets over and with a voice that must have sounded quite pompous and officious said: 'Please deliver them to the desk at Stuttgart. You will be able to leave now. Everything is OK.'

As I turned away and took my lonely seat on the coach I heard the roar as the first engine powered into life. What a God I had. I was amazed ... he had delayed one hundred passengers to keep me from trouble.

Back at the airport Reuben stood waiting with a knowing grin all over his dark face. 'The plane didn't go, did it?'

'Of course not,' I replied, unable to keep the smile from my own face, although at the same time feeling shaken by the miracle which had kept a plane from its timetable.

Little miracles were to play a major part in my life. Some weeks later I was at Frankfurt again, bothered by a spiritual problem, and wanting to telephone Peter in London to talk over the phone. The call used up all my money. The counsel was wise and spiritually lifted me – but it wasn't going to feed

me, and I was hungry, having missed one plane to Stuttgart
and knowing that the next was some hours away.

I sat in the airport lounge, closed my eyes and prayed.
'God I'm so hungry, I haven't eaten for two days. But I
needed to make the phone call, you know that. Please make
someone drop some money and not realise it, so that I can
eat.' It was a stupid, unrighteous, prayer. And God was not
going to answer such an idiotic request . . . at least, not in my
way.

When I opened my eyes there was no money on the floor.
Instead a woman was walking towards me purposefully.
'Where are you going to?' she asked.

'Stuttgart.'

'Oh, so am I. I have just missed my plane and now have to
wait for the next one. I don't want to wait for two hours here.
May I invite you to join me for a meal in the restaurant?'

In the restaurant she told me to order what I liked. 'I'm
paying,' she said.

I really did pray over that meal, praising God for his
goodness.

As I opened my eyes she was looking at me. 'That was a
long prayer – are you a Christian?'

She sat enthralled as I gave her my testimony over the
mealtable – including God's answer to my prayer.

And there was another demonstration of God's goodness
when I arrived home. The next morning in my mail I
received a cheque from a cousin for exactly the amount of
the telephone call.

I enjoyed flying with Lufthansa, seeing the world – but a
far greater thrill was my work with the church and
particularly with young people.

The coffee bar was going well with an increasing number
of drug addicts and depressed teenagers coming along. They
would listen to sermons and talk until late at night with often
up to a hundred present. But we didn't confine our
evangelistic activities to the church. The streets of Asperg
and surrounding areas were full of needy people and
nowhere was the need greater than in the red light district.
The area was a haven for evil, full of night-clubs and discos

where the youngsters could become entangled in all sorts of crime and depravity. But I was determined that God's Good News must go there as well. Over the course of a few months I got to know the managers of a number of night-clubs and had their agreement that I could go to the clubs to talk to customers – providing I wasn't a nuisance.

It was eleven o'clock one night when I was praying with a friend and we felt we should visit a certain club. Inside we were drawn to a man sitting alone at a corner table. We stood and asked if he minded if we sat with him. He answered in English, saying he was an American serviceman. 'What do you want?' he asked with the sort of smile that suggested he knew the answer.

He wasn't ready for what we told him, however. 'I'm a Christian and want to talk to you about Jesus Christ,' I told him. 'I know that Jesus loves you and believe you need him.'

He went pale. His eyes filled with tears.

He spilled out his story. He was just back from Vietnam. His father was a Christian minister and he himself had been a Christian before being drafted to Vietnam. Sex, drugs and killing during that vicious war had robbed him of his faith and he was in the club drinking to gain enough courage to commit suicide.

I told him about the times when I had reached that same low ebb and had tried to take my own life. Then I explained how Jesus had forgiven me, made me a new creature and given me a new zest for living.

The Vietnam veteran broke down. Head slumped over the table he sobbed out how he had told God earlier in the evening that, if he would forgive him and give him one more chance he was to send someone to talk to him before midnight. I looked at the clock – it showed minutes to spare...

We continued to talk when the owner of the night-club came over, obviously suspecting that I was a prostitute chatting up a customer before taking him away. 'Who do you work for?' he barked.

Filled with joy at my providential meeting I couldn't resist answering, 'I'm working for God, why do you ask?'

It was time for the club-owner to be puzzled. But the amazing thing was his next action. He took my hand and led me across the dim dance floor towards the disc jockey. He leaned over and had a quiet word with the DJ, who nodded, and then swivelled the microphone round. 'Listen, everyone,' he boomed through the sound system. 'You folk never go to church so the church has come to you tonight. I believe this young woman has something to tell you.' He pushed the microphone into my hand, smiled, and walked off, leaving me to face the flashing, coloured lights and the pale faces staring at me from behind the circular tables.

All I could do was breathe a prayer, 'Jesus help me', and talk for five minues about the Jesus I loved and served.

And that wasn't a unique occasion. The following week in another night-club where a noisy discotheque was taking place the music was stopped for a couple of hours while our team of workers talked about Jesus. We prayed for youngsters who gave up drugs on the spot as they became Christians and began a new life.

The fervency of our witness spilled into the church. The pastor was marvellous, encouraging the youngsters who came in and giving me the freedom to hold Bible studies and even speak on Sundays without formal training.

My parents didn't like my religious activities. They couldn't understand why I was willing to seemingly waste my time helping dozens of people who didn't seem disposed to receive help. It was, in their opinion, a waste of my free time. But even they began to admit grudgingly that things were changing in the area. I walked the streets, talking about Christ to anyone in the clubs, or at the tables that spilled on to the pavement from cafés and pubs. During the day I was in my Lufthansa uniform; at night I slipped into a trouser suit for the work I considered more vital.

For three years the work progressed, with many young people discovering a new meaning to life through Jesus. They were exciting times. Often we would discuss Bible topics into the early hours.

On one such occasion the subject was 'holy anger'. I didn't believe such a thing was possible and made sure everyone knew my views. Back home at the flat after the meeting I entered as my parents were arguing loudly – at least father argued, mother sat in silence while he raved. I stood on the balcony while the noise raged. I prayed: 'Lord, what can I do to stop it? It hurts so much. I can't cope with it any more.'

All my life I had been afraid of my father, and even after we became friends I still felt at a distance when he was angry. Suddenly something snapped inside me. I walked into the sitting room, stood in front of him and shouted louder than he. 'Now will you stop your shouting,' I roared. 'Just what do you want us to do to show you we love you? For years I have cried out for a real relationship with you; a real father. Why do you make it so hard?'

He went pale, dropped into the corner seat and stared at me, speechless. Mother sank back in her chair, in fear.

I grabbed my coat from the peg by the door and ran into the night. For an hour I ran, asking myself: 'What have you done? That can't have been holy love ... it can't have been done in love ... why did you do it when you said anger is wrong?'

Battering my mind was the question: Should I go home or have I lost everything I have worked for? Although it was late evening I knocked on the youth leader's door for advice. He sat me down and gave me his little daughter to hold. Just cuddling the tiny body calmed me down. He read me the story of Jesus in the temple ... Jesus full of holy anger clearing out people who were doing wrong. It helped to see that Jesus got angry. Condemnation left me and I returned home.

From that day my father respected me as an adult woman; I was a little girl no longer. And the arguments stopped in the house while I was present. Men I knew who worked with my father took me aside in the street one day to ask what had happened to him. 'He's changed. He even told us he'd made many mistakes and was sorry,' they said. 'That's unheard of.'

The change didn't count for much during our Christmas service, though. I had invited my parents for the traditional carol service. Although many prayed for my father to come, I was still surprised when he turned up. But very quickly my surprise turned to embarrassment as he staggered into the church, smelling of alcohol and wearing his filthiest hunting clothes. He scuffled about noisily. I felt so ashamed of my own father – it really hurt me. 'Why can't my family be normal?' I pleaded in prayer.

But that was not my only concern at the time. Manfred, the young man from the youth club, had seen my father in that state as well. I liked him very much, and was afraid that he would be put off by my non-Christian parents – especially after my father's bad behaviour. Partly because of my home-life and the desire within me to have a home of my own, I wanted to get married. Yet it seemed I was my own worst enemy when it came to attracting the opposite sex.

My feelings for Manfred continued. We had a good relationship, talking for hours, but we were both very shy. We had known each other for seven years when I finally plucked up the courage to demand a straight answer. 'Will our relationship ever lead to marriage?' I asked.

Poor Manfred. He looked blankly out of the window (we were sitting in my car). 'I think you are too competent for me,' he said in a stilted voice. 'I don't know where God is leading but I don't think I could be by your side when you get there. You need a Billy Graham, not me.'

It tickled my pride a little, but only later when I had recovered from the hurt. As he left the car I drove round and round the area at speed like a maniac crying my heart out.

And the hardest thing to bear came a few months later when a new girl moved into the area and fell in love with Manfred. I had to watch their relationship blossom and develop. This dark-haired, beautiful Christian girl knew nothing of my feelings. Painfully, I realised she was better for him than I was.

It was still an emotional strain, however, and precipitated more gall-bladder trouble, pushing me into hospital for six weeks for a series of painful treatments. Even that gave me an opportunity to see how loving and caring my Christian friends were. Every day for six weeks they visited me, bringing flowers and presents, or coming to pray and encourage me. And none more so than the Methodist minister.

The demonic attacks which had robbed me of sleep for much of life sparked off fresh trouble in hospital, where the nurses noticed how restless I was at night. I was sent to a sanatorium to rest; they had perceived that something was wrong but I didn't want to discuss it with anyone. My Christian life seemed at such variance with the dark world which descended at night and at some other moments when I was alone, that I had kept my fears bottled up except for the times I could share them with Peter and Reuben.

But the sanatorium I was taken to was in the Freudenstadt area of the Black Forest – a district noted for its occult activities. I sensed the evil powers as soon as I arrived and each evening went berserk, shouting and screaming into my pillow as the black shadows, noises and moving objects threatened my sanity.

Some of the nurses tried to be helpful, coming to my room at night and giving me drugs and injections to help me sleep but the only effect was to put me back on the dreadful drug-taking treadmill I had shaken off some three years earlier.

One evening I could stand it no longer and took every sleeping pill I could find, and a bottle of gin brought to me by one of the nurses. I couldn't cope with the nightly visitations of demons any longer. All I craved was one night of sleep. I woke to the crashing of the door as doctors burst in.

One man helped me through this time: a local minister who sat with me and prayed for long periods. He prevented the doctors sending me to the psychiatric ward, for which I was grateful.

Something he told me made me realise how much God was trying to help me. The minister was new to the area. In fact as a middle-aged man he had been invited to become pastor of the church and had refused. But something had drawn him later to accept. After he had moved, he had been surrounded by boxes and the usual debris of taking over a new house when the phone rang. He picked it up from its place on the floor, to hear a voice say: 'We don't want you here.' As he put the phone down, mystified, he had noticed with horror that it wasn't connected. The wire led nowhere. The phone had rung and a voice had spoken when it was not humanly possible. That experience with the unseen world meant he understood my fears and frustrations.

Fortunately for me the power of God was stronger. Peter Holmes was praying when he felt a real burden for me. He was in England and somehow God told him I had problems. 'What shall I do, Lord?' he asked.

'Get in your car and go and help her,' was God's reply.

Peter, bless him, jumped in his car at Wimbledon, South London, and drove all the way to the Black Forest, his only rest being the enforced halt on the cross-Channel ferry.

During the evening there was a knock on the door of my small bedroom in the sanatorium. When I opened the door there stood a dishevelled Peter. I fell on his neck weeping and praising God. For three hours Peter stayed, praying and talking. Then he insisted we both knelt by the side of the bed and I prayed, confessing my sins, and asking for forgiveness. I felt a new hope surge within me.

It wasn't long before Peter was on his way, the flash of light as his car's headlights searched the narrow courtyard the last I saw of him as he continued his journey, and I was once more alone. But I had been witness to such an incredible miracle – his arrival – that I knew I was able to face the future. The miracle, Peter's immense love and obedience to God, and the sense of forgiveness I now felt, gave me new hope. I left the sanatorium and went back to Stuttgart. Life was due to begin again.

8

COLLEGE FAILURE

When I returned from the sanatorium, the job with Lufthansa didn't have the sparkle it once had. I was not fulfilled and realised that I could not continue to do two things – work, and carry on all the church activity in which I was engaged: certainly not at the pace I had previously been operating in the two key areas of my life. So the idea of going to Bible college and becoming a full-time Christian worker became a real desire.

I was accepted for St Chrischona in Switzerland – an interdenominational Bible college offering training for missionary work. I arrived on a beautiful sunny autumn day. The college, not far from Basel, was situated in lovely countryside with the mountains in the distance.

If I thought, however, that college was going to solve my problems I soon discovered otherwise. My difficulties lingered on: pain, sleeplessness, and demonic attacks. I could not believe that they could remain in such Christian surroundings.

On top of that was the fact that it was an old-fashioned college with very strict rules which I found hard to keep. Having travelled a lot and developed a free life-style many of the rules appeared to me to be silly. For instance, if I wanted to go out in the afternoon – even shopping in Basel – I had to sign a document, called a visa. It was an irritating and seemingly pointless rule. But what it really amounted to was that we were not allowed out without permission and that was only given in exceptional circumstances.

One evening I received a telephone call from the assistant pastor of my home church. Before going to college I had been praying for, and counselling, a woman in Asperg who, the minister informed me, was now threatening suicide. He considered I was the only person she would talk to and trust enough to help. I promised to visit her the next day if the Lord wanted me to do so. As he hung up I prayed: 'Lord, if you want me to go, please confirm the need, and supply a car and the money I shall need for petrol. And since the only time I can go is tomorrow afternoon, you will have to do something about the girls' club.' Inge – another student – and I were due to lead a group of girls in the village as part of our practical training.

The following morning I received a letter in the post, containing a cheque for ten pounds just enough for the petrol needed for the drive to Asperg and back. The only problems now were the car, and the club. Inge volunteered to drive me to Asperg in her car – another solution – and when we went to the hall to wait for the arrival of the girls, we waited – but no-one turned up. It was amazing; usually the girls packed the hall.

We decided it was as good a sign as we would get, clambered back into the car and Inge started to drive towards Asperg.

I delayed only long enough to make one telephone call – to a student friend asking her to leave a back-door key under the doormat because I knew we would not be back until late.

As Inge drove up the hill in Asperg to the woman's home, alongside the prison, I prayed fervently for help. Her husband was a prison warder and it was his brutality to her that had brought her to the edge of suicide. The pastor was waiting outside. He wasn't very keen to go into the house but agreed to wait in the car with Inge and pray.

The woman welcomed me. Depression, sleeplessness, disease and frustration, plus the beatings, had driven her to breaking point. All of them were problems I had a personal knowledge of so I felt a real compassion for her. We sat down and, after talking about her problems, I suggested praying.

We bowed our heads and I tried to begin; but prayer was impossible, it was as if two iron hands had gripped my

throat in a vice-like hold. I couldn't get a word out. As I
struggled and attempted to speak the woman locked up and
began to cry. 'It's my husband... he's a spiritist...'

Then she stood up and moved round the room as I still
couldn't shake off the steel grip on my throat. Opening a
cupboard just behind me the woman showed me her
husband's satanic paraphernalia, the sixth and seventh
books of Moses, glasses and other charmed items. Then she
lifted the carpet and tugged it away from underneath my
chair – I was sitting in the middle of a painted circle used by
the Satanists to call down the demons.

The grip tightened on my neck and I was frozen with fear.
If only I had known about the satanism in advance – I
certainly wouldn't have entered the house alone. Powerless
to help I realised I was no stronger than the woman I had
come to assist.

The realisation of my own weakness frightened me. 'He
who is in you is greater than he who is in the world,' I told
myself mentally, and immediately felt it was not true. I was
at Bible college, but I was helpless. Would I ever live to serve
Jesus in power and strength?

As the thoughts in my mind got more confusing and the
bands around my neck got tighter the woman became more
hysterical. When the door-bell rang I was surprised she was
able to open it. Inge and the minister walked in. While they
were praying in the car they had sensed something was
awfully wrong. As soon as they crossed the threshold the
pressure on my throat eased and I could speak, gasping out a
desperate: 'Thank you for coming.'

We prayed for the woman but it was all an anti-climax;
and for me the feeling of failure was uppermost, I had been
unable to help.

How could I hope to continue in Christian work? I was
miserable all the way back, despite Inge's efforts to cheer me
up and convince me that we can't always win and can learn
sometimes as much by defeat as by success.

She drove cautiously into the college grounds, parked the
car as quietly as she could and I raised the corner of the
doormat. There was the key. Silently we let ourselves in,

muttered 'goodnight' and went to bed. It was two o'clock in the morning.

When I was called before the college principal the following day I knew my absence had been discovered. Nervously I tapped on the door. 'Come.' I entered the book-lined, musty-smelling study, and saw all the teachers seated with the principal in a semi-circle.

The principal began to talk quietly, outlining my disobedience to the rules in the six months I had been at the college. He pointed out that I had started to wear trousers when the Bible made it clear it was wrong for women. I bit my tongue rather than demand the chapter and verse for this. Nor had I been given them when the offence had first been pointed out.

Then he recalled that I had broken the sacred rule about talking to male students. Again it was pointless to respond. He knew that the young man was a friend from my own church – we had actually driven to the college together. It seemed so foolish to get out of the car and say 'goodbye' for the length of a term when we were living under the same college roof and saw each other regularly.

Last night, the principal assured me, was the last straw. 'Gabriele, I don't know what will become of you. You are so restless, so wilful, so arrogant. I cannot see how you can fit into full-time Christian work while you remain like this. You must learn to be a servant... you are much too rebellious and we cannot countenance that here. We are advising you to give in your notice.'

It was an easy way of kicking me out. They didn't do anything. I considered it mean but had no choice. So I phoned the pastor of my church and arranged for him to collect me.

My efforts at Bible training had failed as dismally as everything else to which I had put my hand. My three-year course had been cut short after just six months.

Fortunately the little Methodist church in Asperg didn't seem worried by my failure. For the next six months I travelled with our mission team helping young people. Drugs were a growing problem among them and I discovered I was a welcome visitor at local schools where I was invited to take part in religious education lessons and also to some of the social classes to talk about my former drug problem.

What was encouraging was that they didn't object to me giving my testimony. 'Anything that will help get the kids off drugs is welcome,' one teacher told me.

Police officers regularly visited schools to talk about drugs and show what the drugs looked like and I found a ready audience for my testimony. There were two girls and three young men in our evangelistic team. I was labelled the converted drug addict and the others sang and played guitars.

I was amazed we didn't bore each other. We would whizz from school classroom to classroom, and then move on to a youth club or church group in a never-ending cycle of speaking and singing. My testimony, although real, began to sound too much the same . . . sometimes I wondered whether I was saying the same thing twice in the one talk – doing it so often was like listening to an echo. But the other members of the team didn't seem to mind – and I could listen to their catchy music for hours. Yet a sense of emptiness grew stronger. Is this all there is to life . . . to mission . . . to Jesus? I wondered. My heart was crying out for more; something deeper, greater, more powerful.

What I did like about this work was that we were invariably taken to people's homes to stay – and I usually shared a room with the other girl in the team. With company I discovered my nightly visions eased off. I had a problem only when alone.

But my cry for spiritual depth and power seemed unheard and as usual things began to pale. One evening after visiting a church youth group I wandered down from the hall into the church cellar where a disco was in progress. When I walked down the rickety wooden stairs I smelled a fragrance I knew only too well: marijuana.

I looked around the smoky, dimly lit room at the kids cavorting round the dance floor or merely kissing and cuddling in the little alcoves created round the walls. The

blank eyes of one group stared back at me while their mouths
moved rhythmically, chewing. On the table in front was a
small strip of blotting paper and I noticed one lad put his
hand over it, screening it from my view.

I knew the trick too well. The blotting paper had been
soaked in hash – marijuana – and was now being chewed.

Upstairs I confronted the pastor. He didn't want to know.
I was amazed. 'It is harmless,' he assured me. 'I'm not going
to stop them – if I do they will not come to the club and we
shall lose the chance to minister to them.'

'Rubbish,' I snapped.

In school the next day I used the incident as an illustration
of how easy it was to get drugs. It was, perhaps, slightly out
of order to mention the church but I did so, explaining that,
even in the youth club, drugs were being passed around.

The next day the minister came to visit our team, furious.
Parents from the school had been told what I had said and
demanded an explanation. He had told them it was not true
and insisted that I apologise. I refused. It was all so
hypocritical. In any case the next day we were moving on to
another area but it started me feeling disillusioned about
Christian life – or at least church life.

My feelings were edged to the back of my mind by the
rapid approach of a summer mission; a large youth rally,
Heaven in Action, with Ulrich Parzany, one of the country's
best-known youth evangelists, as the speaker.

The meetings were booked for Castle Park – an open-air
complex that would take thousands . . . and thousands came.
I was there to counsel after the meetings but was drawn by
some force to the many drug addicts who turned up.
Somehow I knew they were addicts and we had an
understanding – they seemed to recognise that I wanted to
help.

Occasionally my work would begin before the meetings
ended as youngsters, particularly the addicts, who could not
remain still for too long, wandered away from the area
designated for the meeting. As I saw them wandering
disconsolately away I was moved. One girl I saw leave early
attracted my attention. I briskly hurried through the park

and stood in the path in front of her, almost challenging her to speak to me.

She was a drug addict. We talked but I seemed to get nowhere. The next day, however, I was called to a group of youngsters clustered round a body in the park. As I approached they parted to let me in. On the ground was the same young girl; she had taken too many drugs and was hallucinating.

She was terribly depressed. I talked her out of another suicide attempt later the same day and she asked for prayer. As we prayed I felt God's power in action (a feeling too difficult to put into words). Instantly she gave up the drugs and became a Christian. Years later she contacted me and I discovered she was a teacher and still an active Christian. I praised God for that encounter in the park.

There was another miraculous happening during the crusade. If the stress of dealing with a fairly constant stream of addicts became too much I would find a quiet spot in the park and pray alone. Just a few minutes alone with God would lift my spirit.

On one occasion the only place available where I could escape for five minutes alone was the public toilets. I began to descend the stairs about 10 p.m. when a voice burst on my ear. 'Run upstairs back to the main road, quickly,' it said.

I obeyed. It had a commanding sound.

As I reached the top of the stairs I head a scream and four youths waving knives ran from the toilet to lose themselves in the crowd. Two seconds more on the stairs and I would have been the target of their blades.

At the foot of the stairs a middle-aged man lay covered in blood, knife wounds over his badly injured body.

As I mopped his wounds and tried to help while the police and an ambulance were being called I realised just how near to injury I had been. I began to consider that God was still protecting me; perhaps he had something more in store for me. That very morning I had read in my Bible: 'God will spare your life for he loves you.' At the time I didn't understand what it meant. Now I did. I fell to my knees. He had spared my life. He did love me. He hadn't forgotten me in all the turmoil of my activities. Could it be, after all, that I was beginning to discover I could do something useful for him?

9

SENSING EVIL

My experience with the summer mission gave me a new desire to go back to Bible college. Working with the young people who were full-time evangelists had made me realise just how little I knew.

There was a Bible college at Bad Salzuflen – a training centre for deaconesses – which was brought to my attention. It was a Lutheran place but the Free Churches accepted the qualifications it offered, so it seemed a worthwhile investment of time.

I wrote to them and told them about my past – including the fact that I had been asked to leave the other Bible college. They smiled and took me on. The principal was a very strong-spirited woman to whom I took an instant liking.

It was a very theologically based college and I soon discovered that there were no easy answers to the thousands of questions that continually buzzed around my mind. On occasions they didn't even understand my questions – let alone provide the answers. For instance Ephesians 6 and the fight which was not against flesh and blood but principalities and powers – demonic forces. They did not appear to like talking about demons. I was told there was something wrong with me psychologically as I had already been cut off from my past by Arthur Wallis (I had told them that). I was instructed to 'simply stand up and follow the Lord'. I was introduced to some well-known counsellors but the outcome was always the same: frustration. Somehow I battled on.

After a year at the college I was asked to select a six-month practical course. I had heard from Peter about Operation Mobilisation and their need of young people for summer work. It sounded an excellent idea; so good, in fact, that it led me to give up college for a while and apply for a year's training with OM instead.

I went to a conference at a place near Brussels in Belgium with leaders, such as George Verwer and Roy Hession instructing us in personal work. Our training consisted of learning how to go from door to door selling Bibles or religious books and giving away literature when we found folk willing to listen.

The first night was tough and an indication of what was to follow. The conference was held in a disused factory which had been taken over by OM as their headquarters. It had formerly been a tannery and the old leather smell seemed to hang in the air permanently. With another working tannery just a few miles down the road I never did discover whether the smell was hanging on from the past or merely drifting upwind from the other factory. It was situated in a lonely spot, surrounded by cornfields waving their ripening corn in the slightest breeze.

I didn't get any sleep the first evening because of the hard stone floor in the factory. I blew up my air-bed and slipped inside my sleeping bag and lay down until the soft hiss from underneath my body told me the bitter news that my bed had sprung a leak. I was not able to mend it so I spent the first few weeks of my work with OM on the flat air-bed, except for when we managed to get accommodation with kind people on our travels or when someone lent me a bed that worked.

Our travels began after the first week's training. I went with three other girls to Italy, driving an elderly, light blue car. We were directed north of Rome and were to sleep in tents, in the car, under the stars or with villagers – with my broken air-bed my personal companion most evenings.

Our job was to sell Bibles and literature and give away other literature while trying to talk to the people we met about Jesus. We had only a little money for petrol; our food was to come from the money we earned selling. Either none of us was good sales material or we had a tough assignment; we ate rarely and on many occasions only because kind villagers took pity on us. We lasted one whole week on bread and water – quite an experience.

The car was loaded with Bibles and other items and we were sent to the mountainous region.

On one occasion I drove the car up a hill which gradually got steeper and more precipitous. The track narrowed until it only just took the car. I drove with a sheer cliff on my left and a sheer drop on the other side – but nowhere to turn round. Petrified of meeting another vehicle we prayed and kept moving. I did not dare stop in case the valiant little car packed up and slipped over the drop. Amazingly, we didn't see another vehicle. We did, however, discover that the track petered out into a sheep track and eventually a dead end. It was a wasted journey.

My three companions bravely jumped out and I was left to steer the car down the mountain in reverse, perspiration soaking my clothing as I gripped the wheel – my life depending on it – with white knuckles, and kept my foot on the brake. If there had been an accident at least three members of the party would have been spared! The baking Italian sun made the journey worse, but somehow we reached the bottom. At the base of the mountain I bathed in a lake to try and calm down.

The area we were told to visit was in a very poor part of Italy – and also steeped in the occult. People had little money to buy clothes and food, let alone Bibles.

One woman stared through a window as we climbed out of the car in her village. A couple of villagers locked their doors and the woman at the window cried out 'They are angels' and banged the window shut, crashing across a heavy bolt as she did so. We found out later they had never seen blonde hair before and all four of us had long blonde hair. Marriages were usually between villagers and hardly anyone had been outside the locality. We managed to coax the woman down to the doorstep eventually and gave her a Bible . . . a typical gesture of our enthusiasm; we didn't even know whether she could read.

Our tour accomplished we returned to Belgium and

reported on our progress before being billeted in the area for
further training. It was beginning to look brighter. I was
enjoying the work – hard as it was – and was enthusiastic for
what the future offered. They were days when Operation
Mobilisation was beginning to expand. Peter was working
for OM plotting the itinerary for a huge ship, the MV *Logos*,
which had been bought to tour the world with Christian
books and witness. It was obvious to me that Operation
Mobilisation was ministering in the world in an effective way
and it felt good to be part of that.

One problem soon emerged, however, which had nothing
to do with the training but with the house in which I was
placed, living with four others. It was outside a town
surrounded by vineyards – lonely and forbidding. It also had
an evil presence which I could not explain.

I had realised that because of my past I had developed an
uncanny psychic ability to sense evil. It was not only a
frightening gift to have but a lonely one because I had also
discovered that I was unable to share my knowledge with
other people: they rarely understood. Christians, I was
finding out, seemed to believe that Satan was not a real
personality – just an influence for evil. I was discovering he
was real and very personal with an army of demons,
constantly at work.

My weird sense robbed me of sleep in the house. My main
duties were to wash and clean and prepare meals but as I
worked there were some things I was unable to touch. One
chair, in particular, was ordinary to look at but gave me a
shiver and cold spasms when I went near it. Subsequently I
discovered a previous owner of the house had committed
suicide in the chair. And later still I heard that other owners
of the property had been steeped in the occult. Animals had
been killed and blood sacrifices made to Satan. So I then
realised that my experiences were connected but at the time I
interpreted it merely as another mysterious influence which
robbed me of peace of mind, and sleep.

One evening I was aware of the evil presence when we were
praying together and through the window came the most evil
demon I have ever seen, drifting through the glass and

glowering at us. I screamed hysterically like a demented person, broke down and could not be consoled. The team could not decide what to do with me. They paid for a week's holiday in a Christian home in the Black Forest where I was able to rest and think about my future.

It was obvious they did not want me to continue working with them; I was an embarrassment.

A friend, Connie, who I had got to know during the coffee bar work at the Methodist church paid for me to return to England to meet Peter and Reuben (both in England now) for further counsel. I was desperate: I loved the Lord, and loved the mission work, but why was I not able to do it? Why couldn't I have a victorious life? Why did demons constantly face me and jeer at me; why did I have sleepless nights because of the visions and sounds? Why did I get such awful nightmares, which made me afraid of sleep on top of everything else?

Any house with any sort of occult history was instantly recognisable to me – while other Christians sensed nothing. Why, I reasoned, if Jesus was as powerful as I believed him to be, didn't he protect me and rid me of the influences?

What was even more troubling, and sinister, was that if I missed reading my Bible or praying for a day or two, the attacks wore off. If I prayed more and read my Bible efficiently, they increased.

In England, Reuben spent a lot of time with me. He knew a lot about the occult from the black magic and voodoo of his own background in Nigeria. I was to discover much later that his faith was very syncretistic – combining the best elements of biblical truth and a thorough knowledge of the word of God, with pagan concepts and pragmatism. It would be years before I fully understood the enigma of Reuben. Eventually I realised he was a victim of his past, just like I was at that time.

A Baptist minister and teacher in his own country, the former Biafra, he was a very strong man with enormous presence which had attracted me to him. I loved him, but I was also afraid of him because of the strange things he sometimes did. At the time, I shrugged them off thinking it was because I didn't understand everything. I was aware that he knew exactly what I was going through.

Peter was also helpful on that visit and between them they refreshed my spirit and I returned to Asperg to my parents who were delighted to see me.

'Why don't you get an ordinary job, forget all this religious nonsense and steady your life,' my mother advised.

My father warned me, 'You'll have problems getting a job anyway – even worse if they suspect you might go off on another fantasy trip with your religion.'

I annoyed them both. 'I am back today. Tomorrow I will get a job.'

'Don't be stupid,' father remarked. 'You don't understand the job market. Unemployment is high here; jobs are scarce. It will take time to get back into work.'

As they both laughed I repeated my promise.

'You can't go back to Lufthansa – once you leave them they refuse to employ you again. What on earth will you do?' father asked.

'I will pray and the Lord will provide work tomorrow,' I promised. And as they left me in my bedroom I knelt by the bed and began to pray. Throughout the night I prayed, asking for peace and looking for guidance. Tears flowed freely as I realised just how dependent on God I was. Deep down I knew my parents were right – it would be a miracle if work appeared. But I badly needed the mercy and love of God. As night wore on I kept praying until eventually I fell into a troubled sleep, still on my knees by the side of the bed, not knowing what the following day would bring.

10

NIGHT NURSE

The following day dawned with my decision made. I was off drugs so why not work in a hospital? My medical training as a doctor's receptionist and my work in the X-ray department might prove useful so I reported to the local hospital in the Asperg area that morning to look for work.

When I returned home it was to stagger my parents. I was due to begin work the same evening as a night nurse. One nurse was willing to help train me and my former training was acceptable. I was even to be allowed to give injections and help on the wards.

I rejoiced: my parents were amazed.

It was work that I enjoyed. And an added bonus was that because it was night work I had to sleep during the day and for the first time in years discovered what real sleep was like. My visions and voices disappeared during the day. I wished I had thought of this solution before.

Gradually, as 1975 slipped into 1976, I became interested in medicine, ordering a whole series of homeopathic books, since that side appealed to me more than the surgical.

I decided as I watched patients return after treatment, still ill, that often it must be something deeper than organic malfunction; there were psychological influences at work.

I became fascinated by psychology combined with natural cures for the body.

My main problems arose when people died, especially on the cancer ward. It was hard to accept that there was nothing that could be done.

Eventually I was moved to the suicide department where drug addicts who had taken overdoses, and others who had tried various methods of suicide, were brought. I was shocked at how cold and clinical treatment was. When it was a matter of fighting to prevent death claiming another victim we were cold-blooded, pitting our wits against sometimes impossible odds to keep people alive. Sometimes we won; sometimes death won. It was an awful battlefield.

Occasionally the police would bring us an alcoholic to 'dry out' or a drug addict to wean off drugs before they faced trial or went for the term of imprisonment they had been given.

One typical night slipped by with no-one seeming able to sleep. One man in our special room was causing a lot of bother – despite many sedatives. Eventually he quietened down and we thought peace had come. But just after midnight when I did my regular round – every thirty minutes the wards needed checking – I peeped through the little window in the door to see a terrible sight. The man had torn a toilet from its moorings and smashed it into pieces, cutting himself badly. Blood was spattered everywhere; over the bed, the walls, the floor, and he himself was more red than white. When I rushed into the room he called for silence. 'The Indians are coming,' he warned. 'Keep down. They'll kill us if they catch us.'

For valuable minutes I had to play with him, pretending to hide behind the bed until the cavalry arrived to rescue us. It was the only way to get near enough to identify the extent of his wounds. Then it took several phone calls to raise the police and have the man transferred to a prison hospital with supervision.

Even though I was sleeping better as a result of my changed routine, at home the tension was mounting. I was more and more convinced that my demonic problems originated from my aunt; my mother rejected the view, claiming her sister was 'too adorable' to do anything that cruel. In fact my aunt told her: 'I would never have done anything I thought would hurt the child.'

Often mother would cut me off in the middle of a sentence and pretend it was all a joke; nothing was wrong; it was just my imagination. They didn't know what they were doing or encouraging. The occult had been passed down through generations of my family and Satan had deceived them all. Occasionally I discovered scraps of information that pieced more of the puzzle together – mother sometimes talked of her occult connections... she mentioned healings at midnight on nights of a full moon... people who died mysteriously... how she had consulted a fortune teller for fun... To mother it was always a joke, something to use to win a laugh. Even the subject of heaven brought a laugh from her. 'God has created a special gymnasium for me in heaven,' she chuckled.

Unable to accept my own convictions, mother grew cold towards me, rejecting all I was telling her about Jesus and my life with him. She wanted her daughter to be what she had had in mind for her all her life – and Christianity didn't figure in that plan.

She had always retained her own figure and although beginning to age she was still out jogging in the forest regularly to keep her superb figure in trim. On the other hand my figure had retained its tubby appearance. Even as a child mother's slim looks and athleticism sent pangs of jealousy through me. Then she could run faster than my school friends and now her teasing reached greater proportions; the fatter I got the more she teased. On a previous visit to hospital I had been put on a zero-diet for four weeks without losing a pound. I was told I had a hormone imbalance – yet the teasing went on, and my father joined in.

Their words hurt me. They hurt me so much that one day I could stand it no longer and determined to lose weight. To do it I decided to eat nothing until I had a figure like mother's. It became an obsession. A cup of coffee in the morning, another at mid-day and sometimes a third in the evening were all I allowed myself. And I began to smoke as well as taking drugs to lose weight.

It took a great deal of nerve to stick to such a strict diet at first but after a few days I discovered I could keep to it – the hunger pangs were not as strong. It took four weeks for the

full effects of my foolishness to manifest themselves. I
collapsed on duty and for two days was unconscious in my
own hospital.

When I came to the head doctor tore into me verbally. I
was on a drip feed to try and replace the food I had robbed
myself of, fighting for my life. Once again my parents were
shocked and it shocked me. I suddenly realised I had been
playing around with my body again, even though it was in a
different way from the drug-taking I was used to. It seemed
self-destruction was an urge that unconsciously attacked my
mind at any opportunity.

As I lay in the hospital bed I reflected again on those verses
in the Bible that spoke of the body as the temple of the Holy
Spirit, and of how I had abused that temple once more.

Months later I seemed to be well and truly over the
sickness when the craving to ignore food took over again and
I stopped eating. I couldn't face the thought of putting on
even a few ounces in weight. Depression hit me and once
more I ended up in hospital. I had not realised how much of a
hold becoming slim could take on a person . . . it seemed that
I didn't even mind dying if that were to be the outcome of my
efforts. My priority was getting slim.

My body began to crack up, like a car which had come to
the end of its useful life. My liver seemed to stop working
and, because my gall-bladder had been removed years
before, my whole system seemed to be failing.

My doctors, who weren't looking at me spiritually, of
course, couldn't fathom out the reason for the mounting list
of problems. To me it was as if I had signed a suicide pact to
discover what people would say when I died. 'Poor girl,' or
'Why did God allow that?' were some of the words I
imagined friends saying until I began to realise that my self-
destruction was a protest at God for his seeming inability to
help me conquer the demonic forces which bound me.
Physical pain seemed to compensate for the lack of spiritual
strength.

Somehow as usual God's hand was on me. One morning I
woke to the realisation that I had to live. I knew I couldn't
keep on denying Christ in this futile way for I could not

testify to his goodness unless I was prepared to live the life he wanted for me.

But I still seemed unable to live his life and the pressure of that frustration built up. I wasn't good enough for Christ. I wasn't good enough for my parents. I wasn't even good enough by the world's standards. Everything I considered reflected my own worthlessness.

There was nothing else for it but to return to Britain and my friends. I spent a month in Edinburgh with Reuben who was back from Africa doing final studies for a doctor's degree. On this occasion his wife and small daughter were with him and they began to build some fresh order into my life.

For hours too I talked with Reuben, his smiling black face seeming to infuse me with a new desire to live for God. And all the time his care and compassion were soothing my depressed, troubled mind. The love of his wife and daughter began to reach me ... I loved the way that little girl, free from life's troubles, would play for hours.

My questioning of Reuben became more intense. There was something about him I could not understand – and I wanted to unlock the secret. One night he invited me into a graveyard. 'I am going to do something to shock you so much and take you through such fear that you will not fear again. I must break the hold that fear has over you,' he told me.

I felt my hair prickle in my scalp; it was standing on end. 'This can't be holy,' I thought. But I dare not leave. Anything was better than the frightened life I was leading.

Reuben told me of voodoo practices and how the medicine men in Africa practised, painting vivid word-pictures that gripped my imagination. I was even more scared, but his words magnetised me ... he seemed to know all about God and Satan, but my mind was a confused mass of wandering thoughts.

He told me he had been raised from the dead and was one of the greatest and most powerful preachers in Nigeria, telling me he could drink poison and not feel its ill effects. The power within him frightened people. He promised, at some stage, to lead me into many secrets. 'What secrets? And why not now?' I wondered.

I was so desperate for help that I listened, frightened, but anxious for anything that would heal my own deep spiritual wounds. He made me drink a special brew . . . but I refused to go into the cemetery with him. That was more than I dared do.

My month with Reuben began to rehabilitate me but I was never certain whether it was the things he told me, the love he shared, or the friendship of his family that provided the healing. I began, however, to understand more and more of the power of Satan.

What made me feel helpless was the feeling that every time I was in trouble I had to come to England for help. The people at my little Methodist church in Asperg were completely lost when we talked of occult practices and demonic influences. To them it was wild, imaginative talk. Demons had ended with Jesus. The fight against Satan and demons had been won on the cross. That was true but the New Testament spoke so dogmatically about demons and spiritual battles as I read Ephesians chapter six. Perhaps some of the folk did believe . . . but certainly no-one knew what to do. I was only ever told: 'Love casts out fear. Just believe.' And this seemed only to put me under growing condemnation as I felt guilty of lack of love.

Rather than proving helpful Christian books on the occult produced more fear; they explained some aspects, but without a clear hint as to how to fight or escape the occult.

It seemed that I was destined to walk the earth for a lifetime plagued by demons and taunted by Satan despite my love for the Lord. 'How could Satan have been conquered,' I kept asking myself. 'How could Jesus have won the victory?' Or 'what is wrong with me?'

It would be some time before most of my questions were answered. One of my prayers, however, would soon be answered, and in a most unexpected way.

11

FATHER'S HANDS

It was during Easter in 1977 that one of my most fervent prayers was answered. My work at the hospital – despite the time off – had earned me enough money to do the final year at the Bible college in Bad Salzuflen that would qualify me for work as a deaconess. In January I began the final year and at Easter went home for the holidays, working again at the hospital as a night nurse to boost my funds.

But one evening before work I had one of my first long and productive conversations with my father – now aged seventy, and on the surface the antagonistic atheist he had always set himself up to be. My friend, Connie, was visiting us and we talked about Jesus Christ with my father. I explained just what Christ had done for me despite the many setbacks in my life. And as I talked about Jesus as the only way to heaven and belief in his death on the cross as the only salvation father looked me straight in the eye and said: 'Gabriele, I believe in Jesus. I believe he is the only way to God.' I stood amazed, tears welling in my eyes as I rejoiced. Simultaneously we reached out and our hands met. He gripped my hands in his. There was no need for any other words. We didn't even need to hug each other. Our relationship was sealed.

For the first time in many years when I went into my room and flung myself on the bed in tears they were tears of happiness. Connie's arms went round me – she was a great comfort.

I couldn't stop praising God. For ten years I had been praying for the salvation of my father. Jesus had saved him – despite my doubts. God is far greater than fear and doubts – and He answers prayer. Now I knew God was in control.

The next day I returned to college, still excited at God's goodness. Three days later I took a telephone call from mother telling me that father had died.

I took the next flight back to Stuttgart to organise the funeral. Father hadn't wanted any mourners – a request we made sure was fulfilled. For an hour mother and I sat silently in the chapel of rest alongside the coffin holding the last remains of my father.

I asked mother if she would mind if I prayed and this time there were no jibes, no laughter, simply a quiet 'If you wish.' I knelt alongside the coffin, inches from the cold body of a man whom I had only recently come to love deeply as a fellow-Christian. I began to sense God speaking to me and, taking off my shoes because I sensed holy ground, I raised my hands in worship – something I had never done before. Loudly I praised the Lord, with mother sitting mute alongside me. As I praised God it was as if he drew aside the curtains of heaven... I saw my father looking radiant, totally different from his earthly image and yet perfectly recognisable to me.

I praised and sang for quite some time, forgetting where I was. The wonder of that moment was shattered by a scream. Mother, unable to cope with my praise any longer, was shrieking. My stumbling attempts to console her with the picture I had seen and the news that father was a Christian and was now in God's presence only made her screams louder, ordering me to be quiet.

At the funeral I carried the urn myself. As I walked into the crematorium gardens I reflected on the ashes inside the container... the ashes of a man I now knew to be with Jesus. Despite the sadness of the occasion I felt a great peace and joy knowing that father was in the best possible place.

My euphoria did not last long. The day after the funeral mother collapsed because of her nerves and I had to stay at home to look after her. That meant phoning the Bible College and withdrawing from my final year.

And within days I had been taken ill myself – a tumour on my breast was diagnosed. I was recovering after the successful operation to have the tumour removed when another tumour was found, this time in my thyroid gland. Fear gripped me. Another tumour. Was it malignant? Was it cancer? The doctors refused to answer my questions telling me that it would need removing – but not for a few months, to give me time to get over the effects of the previous operation.

Would sickness and disaster never leave me? Sometimes I wondered what the point of living was at all? Where was the life more abundant? Only mother kept me alive – she needed me.

Because my Bible college course had collapsed I determined to fill in the time before the operation with something useful and a three month counselling course came to my attention. It was a Lutheran course which would give me qualifications which were acceptable in most churches in Germany and would increase my chances of getting a counselling job. Also, the qualification automatically increased the wages offered by churches. So I decided to go.

It was a valuable three months. The basic premise was that the more you understood yourself the more able you were to help others. Every day we had practical sessions in the nearby mental hospital, which widened our horizons immeasurably. I was delighted eventually to obtain the qualification I had sought.

12

MIDNIGHT MISSION

With the course behind me I went into hospital for the operation to remove a growth from my thyroid gland. The tumour was taken away and for a time I was left to survey the walls of the intensive care ward feeling ready to die, but beginning very slowly to realise that someone was watching over me. God's hand on me was a fact that was gradually becoming evident.

The operation was at the end of March 1978, and my recovery left me with the problem of what to do with myself. I was qualified for an unusual range of things – working in the airline business, night nurse, medical secretary, and counsellor. But I wanted something that would help others and develop my Christian life. I was feeling stronger, spiritually, and the times I had to flee to England into the open arms of Peter or Reuben, were getting fewer. I began to feel I could manage to face life at last. It was true that the night-time terrors had not left me, and I still had demonic attacks when I was alone. I sensed that evil was being induced from a distance and being very specifically targeted on to me, but I was coping better.

Then I met Mr Walter Meng, a short, portly man with a brisk, businesslike voice, he also had a kindly disposition and was the chairman of the Stuttgart City Mission – which included the Midnight Mission, an organisation that had been defunct for five years, without a leader. A businessman, he had the heart of a father and a real love for people, expressed in his keenness to re-open the mission's work among the down-and-outs, prostitutes and drug addicts of Stuttgart.

As we chatted over a coffee in a little café beside the city's bustling pedestrian precinct leading down to the station, he waved a hand out towards the streets. 'I'm tired of seeing nothing done for these people. We must revive the mission and reach them with the Gospel of Jesus Christ.'

His words touched a chord in my heart. I began to feel his burden. He assured me my training – patchy and cut-short as it was – was sufficient. In fact Mr Meng insisted that I could continue my training part-time in a nearby Bible college run by the Lutheran church. I was delighted.

To be working near home and my mother (who still needed me even though she was loath to admit it), and to be able to do work which was challenging, and to complete my education could be an answer to prayer, many prayers.

I visited Munich to see how similar work was done there and as I walked along the street with a Christian friend, who had been working among the prostitutes for years, I realised what a camouflage the brightly lit shops presented. The girls who stood around outside the shop windows looking for all the world as if they were admiring the wares were, in fact, displaying their own. I was introduced to some of them and began to feel a deep compassion.

One girl held my hand and kept it in her firm grip, staring into my face. Heavy mascara lined her eyes and made her eyelashes look like thick bristles. Her face was lined and pitted – evidence of the profession she was engaged in. But her eyes bored into mine and she spoke gently. 'You will never make it as a missionary here, you are psychic yourself. You are too sensitive.'

I looked directly into the deep blue pools of her eyes and felt paralysed. But something within me wanted to reach the girl. She looked no older than I was. 'I love Jesus,' I told her. 'He will help me. Don't worry about me – it is you who needs help from the Lord.'

For a second I knew that she understood – before she giggled like a child caught playing a silly game and walked away, calling over her shoulder; 'Oh, you Jesus-freak.'

In Heilbronn, a nearby town, I visited the leader of a similar mission to see how I could understand the prostitutes better and discover methods of reaching them. The leader regularly visited 'her girls' and took me to one house where about thirty plied their awful, degrading trade.

We went from room to room with most of the girls sitting by the open doors waiting for customers, chatting and talking about Jesus while they slumped about in their underclothes, some obviously high on drugs, others sipping a glass of spirits to keep their confidence up. The talk was one way – the girls preferred earning money to talking about Jesus.

There was a flurry from one of the rooms on the right. The door opened and out came an immaculately dressed man carrying a briefcase, with his hat in his hand. He was looking backwards into the room smiling his appreciation. As he turned on the carpet of the large entrance hall he suddenly realised my friend and I were there. Seeing us dressed as we were and with Bibles in our hands, he must have had a terrible shock; he blushed bright red and hurried through the door to lose himself on the street. I was told he was a local judge – in the daytime he fined the girls and in the evening he used them.

I was appalled. What double standards. 'Lord, why do we try and reach these people for you to see them changed and brought into a society that doesn't seem much better than they are?' There was no instant answer. In fact in the five years I worked with the mission in Stuttgart I discovered that even some ministers, with sexual problems at home with their own wives, used prostitutes. It made such a mockery of the faith we proclaimed.

I began to puzzle over how to reach these girls. If I were working in an office and someone came in from the outside talking religion I would probably be offended if I weren't a Christian. What gave us the right to come into these girls' working places and talk to them? The only valid reason would be a real love for them that was inspired by God. 'Lord,' I questioned, 'what can I say? And how can I say it? What can I do? And how can I do it?'

In Munich I had another experience which threatened to put me off my new vocation. I was taken to visit a prostitute working in her own house. She catered for perversions and had a room decorated with all kinds of torture equipment used to please the idiosyncrasies of her customers. Chains and whips hung on the walls, ropes and manacles were fastened to the corners of the bed and around the room were also dotted artefacts of witchcraft. I forced myself to drink the offered cup of coffee before escaping into the fresh air, breathing in huge gulps of it in an effort to clean my system from the filth inside that room.

I realised that I must accept my limitations, and that I could never hope to do this kind of work on my own. I couldn't visit that type of girl. Either I would have to reject the mission, find another way of doing the work, or discover an alternative. I couldn't conceive how I could keep up with visiting such people without getting tainted and bruised spiritually by the encounters.

I returned to Stuttgart praying each step of the way. I asked God to speak to me and show me a clear pathway. The road ahead was even more clouded when Peter kindly wrote to me and offered me a job with a mission in which he was working in Bavaria. It was located in a beautiful spot. There would be a regular wage, opportunities to travel – it was a tremendous temptation.

Bavaria – or confirm the work with the mission? Walter Meng was a lovely, caring man and sensitive to the needs of others. He offered me a two-week holiday with expenses paid – on top of my normal holiday allowance – to give me time to pray and think.

But as I walked the streets of my beloved Stuttgart trying to make up my mind, I couldn't escape the little voice that kept speaking inside me: 'I am all you need. My strength shows up best in weak people – trust me.'

I couldn't ignore the voice of God. The night before I was due to contact Mr Meng, Ursula who had first led me on to the Christian pathway, phoned me. She wanted to tell me she really felt I would be the one person who could take on the Midnight Mission. She would be praying for me, she promised. It was too much. I couldn't refuse. When I met the Mission's Board of Reference the following day it was to tell them that I would accept the challenge.

Now I had a new job and an enormous opportunity. I was offered a one-room flat in Stuttgart and within hours of accepting was busy touring the shops buying furniture and kitchen equipment. I was in business – and living very near my parish.

One of my first jobs was more pleasant than the work I had envisaged. It was accompanying Mr Meng in leading a holiday for elderly people in France. As I led the old people on to the coach that would take them on the holiday I began to praise God for the variety of experience I had. My nursing training was invaluable, helping with their ailments; and I was able to spend time caring and listening to their problems, praying with them. In the mornings Mr Meng or I would give a short thought from the Bible and we led a devotional time in the evenings. Even my stewardess days were proving valuable as I escorted the old folk around the holiday sites.

The holiday was a brief and bright beginning. Then came the work. For weeks I spent each day walking round my place of work – the centre of Stuttgart – trying to contact the prostitutes and pimps and other needy people.

Somehow, despite all I had learned, nothing seemed to work. The techniques that had been drummed into me in Bible college seemed fated. One night I simply threw myself on God and cried out: 'Help me, Lord.' I left my little flat and made straight for the red-light district. I aimed directly for the first girl I saw, smiled and said: 'Jesus loves you and you are in need of his help. That's why I am here tonight.' She looked at me with amazement.

I was to find the direct, honest approach much more disarming – and more rewarding. I determined not to be 'clever' with my preaching, but to present Jesus honestly and openly, letting people know I was no better than they – a weak person who loved a strong Lord.

As I walked the darkened streets I began to feel bold for Jesus. It was a boldness that was tested in the early hours of the morning when I was finishing my 'tour' and returning home. I turned into a narrow, dark alleyway, to be confonted by a man who muttered, 'Come with me: I pay very well.'

I answered: 'No. I'm a Christian, and the reason I am here at this time is to tell you that Jesus loves you and wants to save you and help you.'

He burst into tears, pushing his hand into the pocket of the overcoat hanging around him and drawing out some papers. Thrusting them into my hand he gabbled out an explanation while I read his prison discharge documents. He was, he said, a murderer who had just finished a fifteen-year sentence. 'Can God forgive me after what I have done with these hands?' he pleaded.

He held his hands under my nose and explained he had strangled someone. Helpless I called out to God. 'Lord what am I to do now?' The answer came with an Old Testament illustration. I told him the story of Moses and how he had killed an Egyptian and still was used by God to lead the children of Israel out of Egypt into the Promised Land. The words sank in and in the alleyway, with dustbins and darkness all round he found the way to God. I was able to give him an address for further help as well. It was a seal on the work I was now positive God had commissioned me to do.

October brought cold and rainy nights on the streets – but more encouragement. I was in my little office one afternoon when the phone rang. Picking it up I was surprised to discover the caller was a former prostitute. She told me how she was now married with two children and that the turning point in her life had been years before when a missionary stopped her one night on the street and talked about the Lord. 'It was a long road – but I have walked all the way,' she said.

I don't know why she rang me. I didn't know her. But it was a thrill to think that God encouraged her to give me that word of witness at that time. I knew then that the sleepless nights, the hours of prayer, and the endless rebuffs on the street were worthwhile.

The most difficult part of the job was not seeing the results very often. I now realised I was just asked to sow seed . . .

probably others would reap. God's word to me that evening was: 'Gabriele, be faithful. Trust me and I will bless your work.'

During October, November and December I busied myself doing God's work in the Midnight Mission. It was a hard, constant battle, but one which I waged knowing that God was able to be victorious.

As December drew on, however, my back became bad with lumbago – was there no end to the physical problems satan was inflicting on me? I knew that Reuben was now in Nigeria and had invited me for Christmas so I pooled my holidays for the current year and the year to come and had an extended holiday over Christmas and the New Year.

I hoped the sunshine of Nigeria would ease my back. The pain was so intense when the holiday date arrived that I had to book a wheelchair to be taken to the aircraft. It was embarrassing being wheeled out to the plane – an ex-nurse and one-time stewardess! I was praying that in Africa it would heal. I couldn't imagine what would happen when I arrived in Nigeria if I were still unable to walk.

My mother and others warned me I was being idiotic – I would be better staying at home and putting my trust in the medical authorities than in people thousands of miles away who might pray.

Strong-willed as ever, I boarded the plane, determined to see God work in Africa. Fortunately my friend Connie from the Methodist church came, so I knew I would have some help. Reuben met us at the airport in Lagos and we stayed with a cousin of his overnight before travelling into the bush to his village.

When we arrived at the 'bus stop' the following morning at 5.00 a.m., it was to find it already surrounded by people. And when the bus arrived it was a case of battling with the masses of bodies to try and get on board. Fortunately Reuben managed somehow to conjure up seats together beside a window; but that was only partial comfort. The bus, a springless, rattling coach well past its reasonable life and with an engine that thundered as if every wheeze were its last, was jammed with people. There was even a clucking supply of live chickens in crates at the back.

For the whole day there was no water – nor toilets! When it came to the latter the Africans just squatted beside the coach when it stopped. We couldn't bring ourselves to do that, so prayed fervently that the whole course of nature would be delayed so we wouldn't need to go. It worked.

If I had wanted heat we had it. It was overpowering, searing through the windows. For fifteen hours we shuddered and rocked along, but fifteen kilometres from Reuben's village I could stand it no longer. We clambered from the coach and I sat gasping on the roadside. I felt sick from the heat and the pain in my back was now a vicious drill grinding into my nervous system. I began to question my mental state. Perhaps my mother was right . . . a hospital was the best place . . . why had I acted so stupidly?

Connie and Reuben prayed and somehow Reuben managed to find a taxi. The taxi was in little better condition than the coach but at least the driver took it easier, noting my state, and we steadily ate up the remaining miles to the village. I hardly remember the final part of the nightmare journey – only that I made it.

Glucose drinks and some special African food Reuben insisted I ate ought to have strengthened me. In fact they seemed to give me the energy to feel the pain more. It was a dreadful night; I rolled in agony under the mosquito net, sweating and praying, with Reuben and Connie in constant prayer also.

If I was delighted to see Reuben again I was not certain about being in Nigeria. It was exotic and exciting – but there were enormous problems. The food was one of the minor difficulties. Most of it we enjoyed but I did find my stomach refusing to eat the fish-eyes we were once served. They seemed to stare coldly at me from the soup-pot in the centre of the table. I stared back and refused them – even though I knew how impolite it was.

The Africans were lovely – some had never seen white people before and often Connie and I discovered children running alongside us pinching our legs and arms to discover whether we were real.

Spiritually, however, it was far from relaxing. The nights were as bad as any I had ever known because of the heavy demonic activities in the area. The sweet, heavy smell of the tropics, the sticky heat, and the throbbing of drums had a strange effect on my system. Pain and fear began to grow more acute.

One day on the beach I almost walked into a quicksand and another day I was so cross with God and the world that I went for a walk in the bush – something Reuben had warned me against. As I swished through the undergrowth a native walked towards me with a huge bush-knife poised in his hand. I was petrified – even though he walked by, grunting a greeting to me.

On another occasion Connie and I decided to swim in a river – only to discover later that it was full of poisonous water-snakes. Yet still God looked after us.

Seeing Reuben in his own land, somehow, made him even more mysterious. His house was a constant source of attraction for people coming for help and they all seemed to obey him instantly whether he ordered them to drink some potion or eat a particular food. And he preached on Sundays. It was almost too much to cope with, the extremes of his life, but still I didn't see the real dangers on the one side of his ministry. How blind I was.

He came to my help one day when I was in agony and brought a friend to pray for me. They both prayed and anointed me with oil. I was afraid but trusted them. As they prayed I found myself going into a sort of trance, drifting out of my body. It felt as if I were dying. Connie couldn't understand either what was going on. She told me afterwards she kept hearing sounds as if bones were cracking. When I came to myself I felt weak and rotten and was ill for a couple of days.

Knowing the area was steeped in voodoo I suppose my imagination had begun to run away with me. The seed of fear was sown. Constantly Reuben and his friend told me to let go and allow them to take charge but I couldn't. With hindsight I was glad. God at least kept me from that.

What was strange, though, was that the pain left me and

when we flew back to Germany I felt completely healed. It was only a few days, however, before I broke down in my office with a high fever, shivering and feeling terribly sick, and an ambulance rushed me to the hospital. Once again I found myself in the intensive care unit at the hospital with doctors studying the strange African virus I had picked up.

I should not have been surprised. In Nigeria one night I had what was obviously a malaria attack, being unprotected after discovering I was allergic to the anti-malaria tablets. Reuben rushed me to the nearest hospital – two hours away by car – to get medicine. I was scared when I discovered it was a leprosy hospital but I was even more surprised when I observed that the patients seemed to have more faith and love for the Lord than I had seen in the western world. It was, of course, a missionary hospital and it shamed me.

It was a shame that clung as, fully recovered, I left the very different hospital in Stuttgart some weeks later to begin to get back into work on the streets of the city.

For three or four months – through to August 1979 – I worked in the red-light district of Stuttgart, touring the streets at night until the early hours, grabbing what sleep I could, before going on to do my paper-work and office chores during the day, in an office provided in a huge block owned by the *Evangelische Gesellschaft* – a massive Christian organisation under whose umbrella the work of the mission came.

There was plenty of work to be done. I visited the police station with some of the girls or took them to the doctor, saw them in hospital, and wrote official letters for them.

One particular girl took up a lot of my time. She was a beautiful girl but on heroin and deeply involved in prostitution to pay for her addiction. She was the first girl I took home to my flat, and a friendship developed. It was that friendship which did more for her than any words or spiritual promises. When she was young her mother had told her: 'I wish I had aborted you' – a statement which nearly killed her. If only people knew the power of the spoken word – it can heal but it can destroy, whether meant in jest or not.

I wasn't very happy about using my flat for social work – it was all that I had and was really too small – so we decided we needed a coffee bar in the area of the night-clubs, and a small hostel to take the girls out of their normal environment. But I had no money and no co-worker.

The committee considered the request and eventually agreed. But if I was delighted with that news Satan was quick to rob me of my enthusiasm. He did it in the way to which I was accustomed – robbing me of sleep. One weekend I went to bed very late but could not sleep. As I dozed fitfully I had the strangest dream:

I was walking up a steep hill along a very narrow road. A black car was following me: inside it were my aunt and an unknown man. They were both dressed in black and had a black dog with them. The car caught up with me and to avoid getting run over I stepped to the side, falling down the hill. My tumble ended in the valley, lying on the grass with a broken back. I was calling on God to protect me as the car turned and pointed towards me and began to come down the hill. I was frightened. I could sense the Lord holding me in his hands, however, and I was able to command: 'In the name of Jesus be gone from me.' The car, the people and the dog disappeared backwards into the darkness.

As they did so I woke and was unable to move. I wanted to go to the toilet but it took half-an-hour to crawl there, dragging myself along the floor on all fours, and it took another thirty minutes to crawl back. I could not understand how a dream could have such an effect – or how I could hurt my back, which was very painful, during sleep in a comfortable bed. It was years before I learnt that Satanists can work easily in this way and have even been known to kill people.

For six months I was in agony, with a seemingly endless cycle of sleepless nights; I was forever in and out of hospital, a series of painful treatments ending with the decision that I would have to live in a wheelchair, or have a very painful back operation. Life came to a standstill.

Despite my calls to pastors to pray for my healing and anoint me with oil as was practised in the early church, they all had excuses. No-one would. This was just not

commonly practised. Once more drugs and cognac –
sometimes half a bottle – because my main medicine; vain
attempts to knock myself out rather than face another
sleepless night in pain.

When I discovered that the drugs and drink were one of
the few ways of forgetting the pain for a while, I longed to
drift endlessly on the tide they washed over me. I wanted to
sleep and not wake up. God hadn't helped me the way I
wanted. No-one felt able to pray over me ... the only other
option to drugs was to face hospital and the operation. I
spent three or four months in three different hospitals with
almost unbearable pain on occasions. But, as had happened
before, it came to an end and I went back to work.

I was still handicapped, not by my health now, but by the
lack of anywhere to house the girls who may have wanted to
escape the lives they were leading. One old retired
missionary spoke to me about the problem: 'It is a miracle
when you can find a bed for one of these homeless prostitutes
to die in, instead of letting them die under a park bench.'

She was right. They would sell themselves for a piece of
bread or an hour inside an ordinary house. Otherwise many
lived outside, summer and winter.

Help was so limited. Often I felt I was passing by on the
other side of the street like the useless religious leaders in the
Good Samaritan parable. Seeing and not helping left me
frustrated and with a guilt complex which I found difficult
when I was in prayer. 'What you have done to the least of
these, you have done to me ...' was the verse that kept
coming to me.

It was certainly not because I desired to build something
big that I wanted the extra help and the rooms – but because
the need stared me in the face every time I walked through
the streets. I wanted to reach individuals for Jesus and see
them changed by his power, as Judith was. She was an
alcoholic and her life previously had been full of sex
experiences. But when she became a Christian, freedom
from addiction followed and we developed a lovely
friendship, open and relaxed. She moved into the same
house as myself and we began to help each other.

Things were going well when, in March of 1980, I had discomfort in my breast and went to the hospital for a check. They found another tumour and I was told it was malignant. Three days later, they ordered, I was to report for the operation. On my way to the office I trudged the streets not really feeling part of the world. Only six months before I had had an operation – now another was due. The word 'cancer' paralysed me.

I had been a nurse and knew the after-effects: probably more operations; chemotherapy; sickness; depression and loneliness. Something inside me broke and I walked in tears. I could not face the future. I remembered the times I had delivered the same verdict to other women and heard their accusations: 'Why me? Why not you?' Now it was my turn. All I could do was cling to the knowledge that God had allowed it to happen – there had to be a reason even if I couldn't discover it.

I found my way back to the lonely office and leaned on the desk praying. I needed to prepare for that evening as I was due to preach in a church fifty miles outside Stuttgart and I refused to cancel the engagement, determined to prove that the strength of the Lord was available in such a situation. So I went, and the Lord blessed the evening. People responded to the word and long after midnight I arrived home shattered but excited by the number of people who had spoken to me afterwards, hungering after more of God. No-one knew the state I was in – God gave supernatural strength. He was very good to me.

The next morning at seven a.m. Mr Meng met me in the office and we prayed. As he prayed I knew something was happening within me without being able to explain what or how – I just knew. I had a peace and trust that I thought had deserted me.

Hours later I was in an emotional turmoil as the thought of losing a breast gripped my mind again. I would never be a normal woman. I called a minister friend in Stuttgart on the advice of Mr Meng and asked him to pray for me; then I wished I hadn't. His only concern when we met was: 'A prostitute needs her breast to work – but as a missionary you don't need yours.'

In fact when I went back to the hospital for the operation they discovered the cancer had disappeared – only a non-malignant tumour remained. I was positive it was an answer to the prayer of Mr Meng. While recuperating I managed to write a paper necessary to complete the diploma course I had been doing and which allowed me to be officially accepted as a deaconess, so even that time was not wasted. Within a month I was fit enough for work, still praising God for the fervent prayer of Mr Meng.

Another prayer answered at that time was my request for a coffee bar. It was opened right in the heart of the red light district – a centre from which to reach the prostitutes, drug addicts, criminals and homeless, and even visitors to the city who occasionally needed help.

Now we could invite people into our own place and create our own candle-lit atmosphere with pictures, music, and alcohol-free drinks. It was a warm and cosy place to be in, with little alcoves conveniently arranged round the room so that we could talk freely without being overheard, and there was a small bar, although we received a lot of ridicule for a bar that sold only tea, coffee or fruit juices. More and more guests found their way to the place and I began to see people come to the Lord. At last things were moving and there was solid evidence of ground being won from Satan.

Five months after the coffee bar opened, in August, I began to find it more difficult to evangelise as my satanic attacks got worse. I was preaching 'who the son sets free is free indeed', knowing I was bound by the demonic pressures that had been forced into me as a baby. I realised I could not lead people further than I had gone myself – and something seemed to bind me. I knew I was a Christian – there was no doubt in my mind on that score – and I loved the Lord; but I longed for victory over the evils that constantly assailed me.

I was given three weeks off to spend eight or nine hours a day in prayer and reading my Bible and it helped me a lot. Also I managed to scrape together enough money to pay for

Reuben to fly to Germany to help me further. I still hoped he could rid me of the fear and attacks.

For the first time Reuben and my mother met, during that visit. As he entered my mother's home and I introduced them the strong, bold African suddenly went shy. It was so surprising I couldn't understand it. Where were his laughter, booming voice and gleaming, laughing teeth? In my mind I had determined that the meeting would end with Reuben sorting my mother out – a glorious conversion, and the atmosphere cleared at home.

Instead he was tongue-tied. He simply prayed, laying hands on me, and, although I felt a lot better, I was also disappointed.

For another three months I worked with the mission and the coffee bar. It was a superb combination, one helping the other; the mission work on the streets being enhanced by having somewhere to invite people. And it was invariably crowded with people finding Jesus or at least coming closer to him.

In November I visited my friend, Judith, in America. Judith, the converted alcoholic, had met an American and was to be married in Richmond, Virginia. I always considered I had played a large part in the romance. When they first met my English was so much better than Judith's that I wrote all her love letters. I was also asked to help with the wedding arrangements. In fact it was not until I got to Richmond that we confessed to her husband-to-be that I was the writer. He didn't seem to mind. Instead he thanked God for a wonderful wife and 'a wonderful friend who writes such lovely letters'.

Three days before the wedding we went to church to talk over the final arrangements. When we returned to the house the door had been forced open and many of their possessions stolen. I felt so sorry for them. But they simply trusted God, prayed for the thief, and went ahead with the wedding, a wonderful occasion. I enjoyed myself socially for the first time in years. I took over the kitchen in their house and catered for the guests myself, putting a few German specialities on the menu.

On the way back to Germany I broke my journey and stayed in England long enough to meet Peter, now married, and his wife Mary, another American. I was so thankful for their friendship – an oasis of peace and contentment, and a consistent relationship of love and care. It gave me the enthusiasm to return to Germany determined to see more work done in the Midnight Mission.

My thoughts were not so positive, however, when I walked to the coffee bar at four thirty in the afternoon with a colleague. 'What can we accomplish in this awful area?' I asked, as I saw again the girls displaying their bodies, and the illuminated pornographic photographs outside the strip clubs.

But with each step God seemed to breathe a prayer into my heart, a prayer of health and strength, that would come from him. As we reached the door of the coffee bar two of our girls were already standing in front, waiting for us. They presented me with a silver-foil dish. I opened the package to reveal a cheese-cake. They had made it themselves as an expression of love.

Within minutes of opening the doors the place was packed; someone depressed needed attention; someone near to suicide threatened her own life; an alcoholic was shouting and threw a flower-pot at me, missing my head by inches but shattering the pot against the bar. Two youngsters wanted to discuss 'love, money, and the meaning of life' . . . It was back to normal.

Offers of help were never refused – especially if the help was behind the bar making tea or coffee and freeing us to talk.

Even in our tiny kitchen we needed to be alert for God's timing. That evening a prostitute brought in her own teapot, asking for hot water to make camomile tea – her stomach was aching – and requesting that we take the tea to her club later that evening. She desperately needed attention and love and we were the only ones providing it. Delivering the little silver teapot opened the doors of another club to us and one of us stayed for an hour or so chatting to girls there. The door sometimes needed something practical to open it.

Incredibly, as we later got to know the owner of the club he would sometimes switch off the porn-films so that we could talk more easily – a miracle in itself. It was seed-sowing. We had to trust God to bless it, in his time and in his way.

That evening one alcoholic arrived who didn't even want to come into the coffee bar – he was dragged in by a huge German sheepdog he was taking for a walk. The dog decided to enter and his master had no option, crashing in and bringing the curtains near the door down with him, as he staggered over a chair. But then he listened as we spoke.

A Satanist also visited us, swearing and shouting and ripping down our posters, before flinging cups against the wall. It was then that I desperately wanted what was often missing in the work – male support. God did not let us down. A couple of our girls prayed in their house and we then were able to quieten the man down.

As the tension seeped away conversations began on most tables – and all about God, Jesus and living Christian lives. A man entered, sought me out and asked for a Bible. 'I want to sort my life out tonight – otherwise it will be too late,' he threatened. One of the women sat down with him and began to lead him to Jesus, none too quietly, and as they talked and prayed conversations at other tables seemed to drop and all eyes swivelled in their direction. Others became interested.

The question I had asked myself earlier in the evening – 'What can we accomplish?' – had been answered. God had given a very clear answer. It was after midnight before we managed to leave, and then it was with a prostitute on our arms, coming for security to our flat as the pimp she had been working with had threatened to kill her. When she was safely asleep in the guest-room we sank into our beds. Another night was over and God had proved victorious in so many ways.

We needed God and knew it. It was never more evident than a few nights later when an American serviceman forced his way into the coffee bar. Drunk, and reeling from drugs, he was shouting and swearing, trying to push me away. We knew he was armed (he had been to prison for doing grievous bodily harm). I was scared but had to do something. It was my responsibility. It was also the night when the few men we had on volunteer duty decided not to interfere. One of the girl helpers started to pray and a customer looked at me with a sly grin and said: 'Only God can help you now.'

God did, but it took every ounce of strength and courage I had to usher the man outside. On the street I could only cry to Jesus to help me – I had no idea what to do, petrified as I was by the gun the man carried. As I was calling on God, assistance came from an unexpected source. Another man from the underworld appeared alongside me, took the soldier's arm and boomed in his ear: 'Come with me, sonny. Leave the nice lady alone.' How I praised God for help – even if it did come from 'the other side'. I suppose it was a mark of the respect people in the area had for us.

On another evening a prostitute entered and collapsed on the floor. We called an ambulance to help her. Two hours later she was back, having run away from the hospital. I sat with her to listen to her life story. She spoke of how her mother had nearly killed her, torturing her by sitting her on a hot stove; and stubbing out cigarettes on her body. Her father did the same. Every man she met ill-treated her. She showed me the marks of her suffering – scars all over her body. As I listened and looked I could not keep tears from my eyes. I called on God for wisdom but even as I wept it was the tears that God used to reach her – no-one had shown her compassion before. She left with our prayers that God would take over her life.

My mother was beginning to respect the work as well, although reluctant to admit it. She was worried about her daughter and came to 'cheer me up', she told me, and took me to a local garage to buy me a present – a new car. A bright red Volkswagen Polo GT in the window of the car salesroom took my attention. My mother signed a cheque and I told them to deliver the car to the house two hours later. They did.

My friends could hardly believe it. I drove as if it were made of eggshells. My friends chuckled as they watched me sticking to speed limits – something I was not renowned for doing – and driving in a fashion very different from the rally-style motoring they had seen previously.

Even so, a week later I had an accident. I had three friends in the car at the time (at least they were able to testify that it wasn't my fault) as I was driving along the long straight road leading into Stuttgart from Asperg. I drove past a man leaning over the bonnet of his car apparently working on the engine. Then I eased down the gears to pull up at traffic lights. As I stopped I glanced in the rear-view mirror to see to my horror the same car careering towards me. All I remembered then was a terrible bang, being flung about and waking up to the fact that my beautiful car was anything but that! I had shock and whiplash, ending up in hospital yet again. The only good things about that afternoon – apart from not being more seriously injured – were that a police car was stationary at the same junction and witnessed the incident, and that my friends weren't injured.

It created another question for which I had no answer. Why an accident when I had done nothing wrong? Why was my new car so badly damaged and I in pain again? Was there a way out of the vicious circle in which I was trapped?

As time went on I thought back to the occasion in London when Peter and Reuben had been convinced that Satanists were trying to home in on me to bring danger and distress to my life. It seemed the only answer to a very complex puzzle.

If some things seemed difficult – others were going well, the years were slipping by and the coffee bar work was progressing. Volunteer helpers were always around – especially at times when I was ill or on holiday. I was grateful for that extra help.

One holiday which did me good was a change from the annual trip the mission arranged for some of the elderly people in Stuttgart. It was decided to take a party to Israel – and I was asked to accompany them. It was a tremendous thrill to walk beside the Sea of Galilee and through the dusty streets of Jerusalem just as Jesus must have done two thousand years before. And it was exciting to be able to use the places we visited as a vivid picture story for the old people, making the Bible come alive as they were taken to Bethlehem, Nazareth and other Bible places.

Mostly, however, it was the hard grind of coffee bar, office work, or pounding the streets of the red light district praying for wisdom and the right words for each occasion.

The mental pressures mounted. My night-time demonic visits continued when I was alone, to make me more perplexed – especially when I was working for God and seeing success in his name. It did not seem to add up.

But what I did not know at that time was that my past had not completely been dealt with. I did not understand the Christian life fully or realise that God wanted to meet specific problems in each of his children. If there was or had been occult involvement (by a personal act or as a victim through the family line) and demonic powers were at work, oppressing, tormenting, or possessing, a ministry of deliverance was needed. The demons had to be cast out. It was not enough to confess occult sins and be forgiven; it was not even enough to renounce it and be cut off from it; once a demon had been allowed to enter a life and get a hold, it needed to be cast out in the name of Jesus.

I realised that this had not happened to me. I was definitely oppressed by demons, harassed and tormented – they had an open door into my life and body because of those acts done to me as a child. Because I was so young at the time of the ceremonies I was totally vulnerable and unprotected.

In the early days of my Christian life the fight was going on within me as Satan refused to give up his victim, while Jesus longed to set me free. Unfortunately for me, not many people (theologians, pastors, or Christian friends) with whom I had contact had much knowledge or experience of this type of deliverance ministry: teaching was lacking and the practical application nonexistent. So I struggled on in my ignorance.

Work over the Christmas period was very intense – the people seemed to be more open as well as needy. Every Christmas I enjoyed working. In the hospital I had always volunteered for that duty and doing the mission work I loved that time of year. It seemed special. In the hospital loneliness and depression were the patients' problems that I tried to combat, but in the red light district it was even worse.

Prostitutes, club managers, gang leaders ... all appeared to recognise that there was something different about that time of year. As I went round with other volunteers giving out small presents on Christmas Eve the hardened drug addicts and prostitutes wanted to talk about their families, their children, or their childhood.

The coffee bar was open from four in the afternoon until well after midnight and despite an increased number of visitors there was rarely any trouble. We sang carols and read the Christmas passages from the Bible and they wanted to join in.

Before we opened the door each day my colleagues and I would pray. But a group of homeless people forced their way in while we were praying and began to upset things. I got angry and shouted at them: 'Shut up. Put your hands together and pray or out you go.' There was a stunned silence and then one after the other they sat down, put their hands together and began to mutter prayers. It was a quiet evening after that.

Things were not so quiet in the months that followed. It was during my fifth year at the mission that my personal problems began to worsen. The demonic attacks became more frequent and my experiences in the coffee bar got more frightening.

It was as if Satan had suddenly discovered where I was again. Tension mounted with the heat of the summer. I felt like collapsing. Mentally I had had enough. My mind was ready to snap. A lifetime of night-time attacks, a four-and-a-half-year stint in the real heart of the spiritual battlefield and lack of understanding of my own spiritual situation, welled up like one enormous bubble that threatened to burst. I was determined, however, not to give up. But how long could I last ... ?

13

CRISIS CALL

I found the work in the coffee bar increasingly difficult. I couldn't sleep; the pains in my back were growing more intense (doctors were talking of a second operation); and a growing number of strange people were coming into the coffee bar.

Underworld men tried to stop the work in an effort to buy up the valuable site for yet another night-club. They offered me money to switch from being a missionary to prostitution. I refused but had no sense of victory.

Witches began to call, telling me they were praying against us and asking Satan for success. 'We shall win,' one savage-looking female witch stated. 'Satan and we are stronger than you and your Jesus,' they taunted me. Unfortunately, deep down, I sensed they might be right.

Once I went into a night-club to talk to people and suddenly six or seven witches were standing round me. I felt as if I were nailed to the wall, powerless to move and hardly able to breathe. They ordered me to stop because they used the cellar for devil worship. I was paralysed. 'Where are you, God?' I cried out. 'What am I doing that's so wrong? I never seem able to overcome these attacks.'

'He who is within you is greater than he who is in the world,' might have been in the Bible – it wasn't part of my life.

Another evening a group of men, new to the coffee bar, arrived. I began talking to them and giving my testimony when there was a phone call. When I had dealt with it I returned to the table and to the conversation. They were so polite and nice I began to feel at ease. It took a while for me to discover what had happened – one of them had dropped some drug into my coffee and soon I was feeling sick and dizzy, with the scene drifting in and out of focus.

The men left, laughing, and I knew I was dangerously high again. Willpower – or perhaps simply the fact that in the past I had been used to drugs – gave me the energy to reach my flat, where I collapsed onto the floor.

Hours later I drifted back to consciousness and managed to drag the telephone onto the floor and ask someone from the mission to come and help me. I was taken to a home and cared for for three days. My doctor was called, gave me valium, and instructed them to make me 'sleep it out'.

The mission wouldn't involve the police, obviously, because they didn't want to be exposed to that kind of publicity, so that meant I didn't go to hospital either where I would have had to explain my condition. As I lay in a strange house, between sheets that didn't belong to me, the tears flowed and I called out to God. I loved my Lord, my mission, the people I worked with ... but there seemed no way I could live a victorious life.

In my desperation I sent about six hundred pounds to Reuben in Nigeria pleading with him to come to Germany and pray for my health and freedom. He came. I pushed all my apprehension about Reuben to one side. I was desperate enough to clutch at any straws.

I stopped taking drugs and slipped into a nervous breakdown. For a week my head hummed and my body craved drugs as the withdrawal symptoms gnawed away at me.

A doctor – a member of the local Baptist church – gave me the necessary sick leave, no medicine and plenty of good advice. And he spent a lot of time talking and praying with me.

Connie and Reuben had hardly any sleep that week as I sobbed and moaned and drove myself on. Connie, a nurse, took a major share in looking after me and the love and care she and Reuben showered on me were deep and real. They didn't know what to do first: treat my body or pray; calm me down, or prevent me jumping out of the window or running away.

One night I cried out for help – an ambulance, anything. Reuben entered the room, laid his cool hand on my forehead and asked me to relax as much as I could. As I tried his hands seemed to become electric with current surging through my body. Soon I felt I had left my body and drifted upwards . . . he seemed to be holding my mind and personality and totally controlling me. From the other corner of the room I looked down on my own figure, writhing on the bed. I was petrified that I wouldn't enter my body again, and that my body would die with no soul and that the real me would be left to wander the earth. Within minutes I fell into unconsciousness . . . to wake six hours later still in a trance, and Reuben ordered me to sleep.

Next day he demonstrated to me some breathing techniques. He explained them well, giving it a biblical reasoning. Later I discovered it was a transcendental meditation technique. From that point I did not feel like the same person. I had more control over my body, and could create strange and interesting pictures which left me with a sort of peace. I could leave the body when I wanted . . . it was like living in another world.

This was in fact the very last time Reuben was to exert such a disturbing influence over me. There was no doubt his love and care had helped me enormously but I came to see that his powerful personality was not fully surrendered to God and this was an opening for the enemy to work through.

At the same time, I was horribly alienated from my mother. When she came over to visit me, anxious to care for me while I was ill, her face seemed distorted by demons. That was the first time I'd ever seen such a thing in her, and I couldn't bear it.

During her last visit she had handed me an envelope. Even without opening it I sensed it contained money – it was vibrating in my hand. I knew that it was possible to put a charm into money to retain a hold over a person and I was frightened to accept it. I realised, however, that I couldn't refuse my mother. Instead I accepted the envelope and when mother had gone checked my suspicions and discovered a hundred Deutsche marks in the envelope. I gave it to Reuben and asked him to look after it in his room overnight. I was afraid a demon would come and attack me, were it in my possession.

Reuben told me the following day, that, sure enough, in the middle of the night a demon tried his door and attempted to take the envelope. Reuben rebuked it and it screamed with anger and left. When he explained this to me I felt so relieved. It was the first time someone else had been affected by the demons. But it still left me questioning God.

'Why, Lord, are you not near me? What is going on and why? How can I escape these dreadful experiences?'

Reuben left for Nigeria when I had recovered physically. Emotionally I couldn't face the red light district of Stuttgart again. How could I tell of Jesus and his love and power when I was powerless and did not experience victory in my own life? I did the only thing I could: gave in my resignation to the mission and just retained the office work for some months while I cleared up my affairs. I was to leave in March 1983.

Before that date, however – towards the end of 1982 – I was feeling really low and recognised the pull towards suicide. My last hope was Peter Holmes. Something told me that a crisis was occurring the like of which, even in my mixed-up life, I had not seen before.

As Peter answered the phone from his home in Bromley, Kent, I pleaded: 'Can you please find a spirit-filled and competent minister who understands the occult and is prepared to counsel me? If you can't, I quit. I can't go on any longer.'

Calmly he replied: 'Don't do anything silly. Give me twenty-four hours and I will have a solution.'

I sat by the phone waiting.

Meanwhile in England Peter was phoning all over England trying to find someone who could help. Then he called Christian Response to the Occult and was put in touch with a man named Mike Costello who would be willing to take me on. Mike was a minister who had seen the seamier side of life and had a lot of experience fighting demonic powers.

Full of hope – and very much afraid – I flew to England. This time I took a week's holiday and was taken to Peter and Mary's home in Bromley. On the Wednesday after my arrival I sat in the back of their car and was driven to Slade Green, on the outskirts of London, in Kent. Mike had set aside a whole day for the meeting. It was an encouragement to feel he cared that much. I was with him for twelve hours.

He heard my story, listened to my endless questions and began to provide answers. For the first time in my life I began to feel that perhaps there was an answer. As he probed and questioned I could relax. He understood. I couldn't understand how a Christian could be demonised, but that's what he said I was. Not possessed – he made that very clear. 'That is something quite different. Possession means ownership and, as a Christian, you are owned by Jesus. But demons can still work in you and hang on to you, tormenting you.

'What we have to find is the open door that allowed them access to you. Sometimes it is a hereditary line, sometimes personal occult involvement, occasionally innocent involvement... or even sin which has become a habit.'

Slowly and surely I saw my need of help. I also began to see that I needed to be willing to seek the help at any cost.

Mike also answered the biggest puzzle. 'Why have I had such trouble when Arthur Wallis identified the family connection and cut me off from them so many years ago?'

'Cutting off is only one part of it,' Mike explained. 'It is the prelude to a longer period of ministry which should include the casting out of demons.'

That was new to me. It was something I was to learn a whole lot more about in the future.

When I returned to Germany I stopped seeing my mother. I needed more time to sort out some of my problems without family interference, I explained, as nicely as I could. She was angry and depressed. Most of my German friends couldn't understand my decision either.

'You should be loving and caring to your mother. How

can you influence her towards God if you cut yourself off from her?' one friend pleaded.

The emotional battle raged inside me. What was the right thing to do? 'What is your will, Lord?' I almost screamed at heaven.

Back to Slade Green I went for more ministry. I was beginning to understand that with thirty-six years of demonic trouble behind me it was going to take a long time to work a cure.

After asking Mike for advice I was prayed for and as I began to feel the ministry acting like a surgeon's knife, digging deeper and deeper, Mike began to tell me he was discovering more and more occult roots.

Like a wild plant the roots had stretched into my being. Fears began to disappear as the praying and teaching exposed more difficulties and they were dealt with. But the more they discovered the more there were. It was as if a cancer were hiding inside me, spawning new evils every time one was taken out.

I began to question Mike: 'How can there be so many demons, and why don't they all go out at once?'

He paused, and replied: 'That is a difficult question, and to be honest, we haven't found the full answers yet.'

But he tried to explain it to me in simple terms to calm my agitated nerves. 'The demonic realm and its ruler are like a spider spinning his web starting with a single strand. The spider adds many more strands to ensure that any insect touching the web will be well and truly caught. The demonic realm needs an opening into a person's life and, once found, it is used as the entrance for more and more demons, forming a satanic web. These demons slowly but efficiently work to bind and eventually destroy a person. The purpose of the spider's web is to trap insects and provide food. The purpose in the demonic realm is exactly the same. Jesus put it like this: "The thief comes . . . to steal, and to kill, and to destroy." (John 10:10).

'The way in which this satanic web is built is through the opening of "doors" in a person's life. These doors are of

many types ... sinful habits can be one. A person – even a
Christian – can fall into a sin again and again until he or she
is no longer in control but rather is controlled by the demon
who took the opportunity to enter (perhaps through drugs,
alcohol, or sexual promiscuity). Traumatic experiences
provide another door – like rape, incest, countless fears,
accidents, death, or rejection, one of the devil's favourite
weapons.

'However, the door that has the strongest influence of all
seems to be occult involvement – one's own personal
activities or those brought upon a person by the family line,
as in your case. This is a direct invitation to Satan to send
demonic powers to work on, and also through, its victim.

'I am discovering, to my dismay, how many of the enemy's
agents can enter a person; but I know also that the ministry
of the Lord Jesus Christ is the way to destroy this demonic
web.

'To fulfil the commission of Jesus we need to cast out the
demons. I have found that this often takes time – in some
cases a long time. Most of us could not cope with a "once-for-
all" deliverance session. It seems that because Jesus loves us
so much, it happens little by little, so that we can learn how
to live in the newly gained freedom gradually.'

Mike then gave me another piece of news: 'Gabriele. You
really need more help than we can give on odd occasions. A
nice elderly lady in the fellowship has agreed to let you live
with her if you want to come to England and stay here until
you are completely cured. We want you to be sorted out
fully.'

The suggestion that an end could be found was all the
inspiration I needed. It was the obvious answer ... quite
apart from the fact that I couldn't afford the air fares to keep
flying to and from Stuttgart and England.

As I prayed about leaving Germany the Lord said to me:
'Leave with empty hands.'

'What does that mean, exactly?' I asked.

'Give up everything you have – give the money to needy
people.'

For the first time I realised just how much I loved my little flat... the kitchen... my television... and my lovely red Volkswagen car.

'Everything?' I asked.

'Everything,' came the answer.

More and more was taken from the flat. A friend bought most of the furniture; Mr Meng bought the television... and a lot of my friends were unanimous in their verdict: 'You're mad. This cannot be God's will.'

But for once I had a strange peace. In the middle of the turmoil, a feeling of serenity ruled in my heart, so I kept on.

As March drew near I was wary about the second – my birthday. Too many bad things had happened on that day; twice I had been taken to hospital for operations; demon attacks had always been particularly strong and this year I wanted to be in England on that day.

Having been a little over-enthusiastic in giving money away I realised I had none for the air fare to London. I prayed hard for a ticket... and two days before my birthday an anonymous Christian in England sent me the ticket I needed. I travelled that day.

As I arrived at Slade Green so did two Americans: Frank Marzullo and Frank Hammond, authors of *Eight Keys to Spiritual and Physical Healing*, and *Pigs In the Parlour*.

As soon as we met they started to praise the Lord. I looked on in amazement. I didn't know them. Suddenly they turned to me and began to talk to demons. I was totally embarrassed. I couldn't see anything... refused to believe that the sort of demons they were addressing were in me. But strangely it felt like the demons were leaping around inside me... I felt like screaming, and kicking... even laughing. It was a spirit of mockery that mocked everything that was of God, Jesus and the Holy Spirit.

Frank Marzullo looked at me and in a loud voice said: 'God has a purpose for your life. He will use you in the future. You will go and preach and you will preach in power to set captives free. You will pray and preach to prostitutes and they will be delivered.'

Having just resigned from the Midnight Mission that was

the last thing I wanted to hear. I was not keen on that type of work in the future.

The next day was my birthday. Frank prayed for me again and more demons were cast out. I was bemused. It seemed a never-ending roll-call. Some were stubborn and didn't want to leave. I was told I would be ministered to during a conference they were holding at the end of the month. The thought of waiting four weeks after having everything stirred up inside me started unbearable thoughts ... Did I really have all those demons? Is this all real? Have I ended up in the clutches of a wild sect, a strange group who just want to use me?

I was totally mixed up. Still in pain from my back I could not sleep and spiritually was in agony, without peace. All the scriptures about peace were in the Bible – none in me!

14

RETURN TO SLADE GREEN

A few days after my birthday experience I flew back to Germany to continue to sell my belongings and cut off all the ties with my homeland. The money I received was shared between friends. Some of my days were spent in the Midnight Mission clearing up the business that only I could do. As I did so I could not escape the feeling that things were reaching a climax.

More strange things were happening; a lamp fell down from the ceiling and almost killed me; I touched a light bulb and it exploded in my hand, the shock flinging me across the room; I was drinking a tumbler of fruit juice and swallowed broken glass which I was sure had not been in the tumbler previously. I could not feel safe in Germany. I wanted to find a place where no-one would know me and no-one could harm me.

I was particularly sorry for my friend Connie. She was with me on many of the occasions when these things happened and it was hard on her, the more so because I wasn't behaving normally. I was under intense pressure. As usual, she was wonderful.

At the end of March 1983 Connie and another friend and myself were invited to fly to London to visit Slade Green for the deliverance conference. I knew the two Franks would be there. It was something to look forward to – and on which to pin my hopes for a complete cure.

Two days before the flight I collapsed in the flat of one of my friends. They telephoned the folk at Slade Green and knelt round me praying. At the same time the people in Slade Green prayed, binding the powers of the enemy to enable me to attend the conference.

With just one day to go to leaving for London I was packing my clothes when there was a knock on the door. I opened it to find a woman standing there, dressed completely in black, looking very evil.

As the door opened she started to shout: 'I know perfectly well you are going to London tomorrow. Where are you going exactly – tell me. Let us know where you are going.'

I was stunned. I could only give a foolish, evasive answer. 'I have no time to speak now. I have to go to the toilet.'

It was not a particularly spiritual reply. Certainly lacking any authority. And the woman repeated her command more forcibly. I didn't move an inch – I didn't want her over the doorstep of the flat. Again I repeated my nonsensical comment.

She turned on her heel, walked a few yards and disappeared into nothing. It was uncanny. I really was shocked now. I knew the spiritist elements within my family were working against me but this was something with which I couldn't cope.

Later, in London, I was told it was a common occurrence in satanist circles, sending a messenger of hell, an 'angel of darkness' they called it.

It wasn't the end. As we sat in the taxi on the way to the airport I should have been relaxing, knowing I would soon be away from it. Instead I was tense, sensing that something was going to happen to the taxi, and worried because my friends were with me. This was one reason I insisted on travelling by taxi – other friends had offered to take us by car but I didn't want to involve them.

As the car left the city behind and moved out into the countryside an iron ball, the size of an orange, came hurtling towards the passenger side of the car. The driver swerved as it crashed into his wing, gritted his teeth, driving faster. As he screeched to a halt outside the airport he rushed round the car, but to his amazement, found no damage. He wanted to get rid of us as quickly as possible, sensing something unusual. And he kept giving me strange looks out of the corner of his eye.

I dared not give a reason. It was getting more and more

dangerous and far too involved. In a strange way I was grateful the driver and my friends were around – showing it wasn't a figment of my imagination. They had experienced it too.

At Heathrow Airport friends from Slade Green were waiting to greet us. They took us to their home and as I had a headache that seemed to be splitting my head in two they prayed and called on others to come and pray with them. As hands were laid on my head I screamed out: 'Leave me alone.' But even as I screamed I collapsed and they continued to pray.

The next day was Sunday. I sat in church feeling miserable. The torment became too much and, as I boiled inwardly to screaming point, wanting to fling objects at the folk there, I pushed my seat away and ran to the toilet.

Once inside I locked the door and collapsed. One of the men was forced to climb a partition wall and open the door to get me out.

But as I crumpled at their feet they stood round me – a wall of love – and prayed again. I just couldn't understand such love. They hardly knew me – every time they saw me meant trouble but the love kept pouring out like waves of an ocean, never ending.

At that point, as I sobbed and felt the compassion oozing towards me, the spark of hope was born. I knew then that I would get help. And I also knew that the end was in sight. Embarrassed, feeling foolish and wanting to fall asleep and not wake up was my reaction. Theirs was to hug and kiss me and demonstrate their affection.

On Monday the conference started. I made my way to the little church, perched on the corner of one pew and sat waiting. Three small stained-glass windows shed shafts of light over the pulpit and a small table in an alcove. Behind it a plaque proclaimed 'Jesus is Lord' in an old-fashioned pennant shape. A decorative pipe organ took up much of the room on the right of the platform – a neat row of twenty-two gold pipes arching upwards over the dark wood instrument.

I stared round the plain walls of the church while the meeting got under way... singing, praising, praying, and with folk generally enjoying the atmosphere.

Then Frank Marzullo spoke, delivering a powerful sermon with words that are still with me. He insisted the Bible was specific regarding the enemy of mankind. From Genesis to Revelation the work of the Devil and his demons was evident. Jesus' teaching and the New Testament letters left us in no doubt, he went on, that we have to fight and wrestle against spiritual beings which are not made of flesh and blood. They are not impersonal forces either, I heard, but spiritual personalities (Ephesians 6:12).

Captivated, I listened as he spoke of the secular world in which millions and millions of pounds were spent on espionage and getting to know the enemy. 'The more information that can be accumulated about the enemy and his tactics the better equipped we are to fight him,' he continued. 'In God's Word we find a lot about Satan and his demons – who he is and how he works, for instance. He is called the "father of lies" (I John 2:22 and John 8:44), and he cannot be trusted. He is the accuser of humanity and God's people in particular (Zechariah 3:1). He also tempts people to sin (Luke 22:31) and attacks viciously (I Peter 5:8). Satan loves to take advantage of human weakness (II Corinthians 2:11). These are just a few of the ways he gets at us.'

He was building a helpful picture and I began to understand the thread of his argument. Then he turned in a positive direction. 'God in his love, not only tells us who our enemy is and how he works, but he also gives us everything we need to fight him – and to win!' Frank identified the preparation needed, using the armour in Ephesians chapter six as his text. 'Put on the armour of God – and put on the whole armour, that means the character of Jesus. Put on the girdle of truth – well, Jesus is the truth and we need to live truthful lives. Ephesians 4:25 makes that clear ("Therefore each of you must put off falsehood and speak truthfully to his neighbour, for we are all members of one body")'. (New International Version)

To put on the breastplate of righteousness, was next. 'Jesus is the righteous one and through him we learn how to live right.'

Frank pointed out that every part of the armour could be applied in similar ways. Having put on all the armour we were to stand, be strong, and fight against the principalities and powers, the evil beings, the demons, spiritual beings without flesh and blood. 'And when they are inside someone – cast them out!' he concluded.

But even as I was agreeing with him and considering his words he started to pray; people began to scream and fall and to me it seemed emotional and weird. I began to consider, as I had once before, that perhaps I had got mixed up with a strange cult. It certainly couldn't be a real Christian church. In my need I called out: 'Lord, help me.'

I wanted normality and freedom – not more strange experiences. Scared and unhappy, I grabbed my coat, pulled it over my shoulders and ran from the church. My running was no better than my athletic failures as a child, but I ran that night ... on and on, eating up the miles, without stopping, almost fainting through lack of breath but still jogging. As I practically fell through exhaustion I managed to find a telephone box and in despair dialled the only number I thought would bring the help I needed – Peter Holmes. I rejected the thought of calling the Slade Green minister or my friends there.

Peter's response was immediate. 'Stay where you are. I'll find you.' Peter and Mary eventually discovered me, sitting on a low wall near the telephone box. Peter put an arm round me and sat me next to Mary in the back of the car, driving me to their home. They gave me a cup of tea to calm me down.

Deep down Peter was shocked. He had considered that Mike Costello and the folk at Slade Green would have the answers he had sought for so long. Now it appeared I was in a worse state than ever. Even so, his calm voice began to give me a better perspective, reassuring me that what I had seen at the conference, which had disturbed me so much, was, in fact, the reality of spiritual warfare. It was simply the practical demonstration of the fight against spiritual forces and wickedness.

His words brought the peace and courage I needed to

telephone my friends and even though it was after midnight
they came to collect me and took me back to Slade Green. I
knew it was there I would find help. Truth began to exert its
influence over me and I began to realise that my doubts were
a ploy of the Devil to prevent me finding healing.

I missed the following day's meeting, remaining in bed to
ease the pain in my body and clear my head. It was not the
best decision to make: I was struck with more occult attacks
in the home of my friends. I was alone in the house – alone
with the demons.

Determined not to give in, I stuck it out until my friends
returned later, which reduced the manifestations. For the
next few days I was able to get to the conference meetings,
and gradually began to understand more. The final night
was a healing service with a packed church.

I was glad it was to be a normal healing service – I was
wary of the screaming and collapsing that praying against
demons seemed to attract. I was full of hope for a peaceful,
joyful service.

Towards the end of the evening the call was made for those
who wanted to be prayed for to go forward. I went to Frank
Marzullo and asked him to pray for the headache I had. As
he stretched out his hand and began to pray I fell backwards,
crashing into the arms of others. I was placed in a chair and
started to scream and manifest the evil that was controlling
me.

I was encircled by people – unable to escape. Dimly, as I
was screaming and calling out, I heard Frank asking other
people to join him, singing and praying in tongues. 'Sing
songs about the power of the blood,' he said and the songs
began to trace a wall-like pattern round me. As soon as the
word 'blood' was mentioned I went berserk. The enemy in
me couldn't stand the Holy Blood. With screams and shrieks
the demon that had entered me whilst I was in Africa
through the unintentional involvement in voodoo left me,
screaming as it was driven from my body. I lay, a crumpled
heap on the floor. Shattered. But freer and more relaxed –
and rejoicing a little. Jesus was the answer, through the Holy
Spirit he had directed those who had been ministering to me.

The following day I flew back to Stuttgart to complete my affairs there before returning to England permanently. I was delighted that Peter and Mary had offered to travel to Stuttgart, to pick me up and take me to England. They were to drive my car – loaded with suitcases. I had got rid of many of my possessions but like many women I clung to a range of clothes and refused to sell the red Volkswagen – my pride.

It was Easter when we left. I had said goodbye to my friends, the workers at the mission – but not my mother. I had not seen her for three months.

My hesitance in saying farewell to mother was not simply because I wanted to cut ties with the family but because Easter was the time when the aunt from America wanted to visit the family. It was now clear to me that she was the one who had sold me to Satan when I was a few months old, and I refused to run the risk of meeting her.

Later I discovered that she had indeed gone to Stuttgart that Easter. I left with Peter and Mary at seven o'clock in the morning... my aunt arrived three hours later. I praised God I was away with hours to spare.

For six months I tried to pick up the broken pieces of my life. Peter and Mary had invited me to live with them – an offer for which I was grateful. I was allowed to rest and get over the shattering experiences I had been through. He was now working for CARE Trust in London – a charity set up to investigate and work to ease social and spiritual problems and I had the opportunity to help sometimes with some of the office work.

Peter and Mary lived in a pleasant detached house in a quiet area of Bromley just a few hundred yards from the centre of town and yet peaceful. It was a typical suburban setting and the sort of area I was used to.

For various reasons the thought of returning to Slade Green didn't appeal. The neighbourhood seemed less attractive, and I couldn't imagine myself feeling at home there. I had problems understanding the community; a constant language barrier cut me off from them and their sense of humour. My mission experiences and the lifestyle I was used to meant I was puzzled by the insular nature of the

folk there – they seemed to fight shy of social involvement
with each other.

And the services in the church were more than I could
stand. I preferred the solid, reliable German services –
everything in place. At Slade Green it was too free –
everyone seemed to do what they wanted, when they wanted.
They called it worship in the Spirit: to me it was chaos. And I
was hurt when they kindly pointed out that I didn't
understand what worship in the Spirit was. I couldn't release
my spirit in the way they did. I sat like a rock while it all
happened round me. I couldn't even raise my hands as most
did.

I was struggling, desperate to be free and sadly
disappointed when Mike told me that at that time I needed
to allow the ministry that had taken place to be worked out.
He said God had not at that time spoken to him of any more
occult roots. But I wanted to continue until that root which I
knew was there had been prised out.

Despite their encouragement I stood my ground, unable
to sense the victory they felt. There was still a blackness
inside me making me tense. Depressed once more I began to
feel rejected and misunderstood. A cold led to bronchitis and
almost pneumonia and I ceased attending the church. On
top of all this I felt guilty, of letting my mother down by my
continual silence.

Peter told me to telephone her. He was convinced that if I
were not reconciled with her I could not get well again.
Mother answered the phone and I burst out with my
apology. I asked for forgiveness and after we had talked I
began to feel better. I began to recover. Mother started to
write again – the wound was healed.

Mike, at Slade Green, felt sincerely that I should get rid of
everything that was from my mother and family. We began
to discover that certain objects given to me by my family
were charmed and affected me, so more and more of my
belongings went.

Mike explained that spirits can indwell or affect buildings
and objects. He reminded me of stories I had heard of
poltergeists moving objects. Opening his Bible he showed me

Deuteronomy 7:25, 'the images of their gods you are to burn
in the fire. Do not covet the silver and gold on them, and do
not take it for yourselves, or you will be ensnared by it, for it
is detestable to the Lord your God.' (New International
Version) Then he turned to Ezekiel 13:18, 'Woe to the
women who sew magic charms on all their wrists and make
veils of various lengths for their heads in order to ensnare
people.' (NIV) Isaiah 4:7 made it plain, he pointed out, that
we are under a curse if we are involved in sorceries or using
the power of spells.

So I started to realise that if an object had been used in the
occult or as an idol to be worshipped it could have a negative
effect on me. Later I was to discover how often investing
objects with magical powers was used by practitioners of the
occult – with the purpose of keeping their subjects bound.

During the spring I was invited to go to the Bethany
Fellowship at The Hyde in Haywards Heath, Sussex. I had
heard of Colin Urquhart, one of the leaders, and decided to
go. It was a beautiful mansion – surrounded by lovely
grounds, and the people were friendly. For some reason I
seemed to understand their English better as well. I went
there regularly. Once more, although I didn't know it, I was
on the run. I hardly seemed to stay anywhere for very long –
job, home or church.

More demons were cast out of me over the months as a
particular couple began to counsel me regularly. Healing
prayer was made and for the first time I began to understand
and soak up the worship, joy and freedom beginning to
infect me as I worshipped – I began to dance and enjoy God's
presence, raising my arms. Inwardly I wondered whether it
was merely because they were relative strangers. I was
curious as to whether the freedom would be with me
elsewhere.

And still, despite Mike's intervention, my mother and I
were in touch. I desperately wanted to see her and be
reconciled ... I fervently wanted her in heaven. Despite
advice I determined to go and see her again. Before I left I
had the most beautiful experience – and it happened at Slade
Green.

I realised that I was wrong in ignoring some of the advice Mike and others were giving me, so I apologised to him and the house group who had showed such concern and love for me. The Sunday before I left I felt I should go further and apologise to the whole fellowship. As the words left my lips I felt healing coming into me... I could feel a new freedom and a fresh peace in my relationship with the people there. Many of the fellowship stood round me praying and praising especially showing concern for my trip to Germany.

There was a prophecy: 'You will see the glory of the Lord. He will be the light on your way if you look to him. You will see his power and might and strength. His angels are around you to protect you and to lift you up.'

With those words of encouragement I was able to return. I packed my cases, stacked them in the rear of the Volkswagen and directed the car towards Dover for the ferry to Ostend, and then Stuttgart.

I had been offered a job as a nurse in an old people's home in Stuttgart – another miraculous provision – and since it was a Christian home it promised great things for the future. I needed time to consider how best to develop a reconciliation with my mother, but felt it would be too difficult to attempt if living with her. This seemed an ideal compromise, since it provided me with a one-room flat in the hospital.

I returned on the Thursday and reported for duty the following day – the first of October 1983. Mother was impressed that I had got a job so easily, and obtained it while in another country. What God was doing with me was beginning to make her think, I could tell, but she didn't want to know about Jesus. She was still the same pleasure-loving person she had always been... uninterested in the real issues of life. In the old people's home I had a beautiful time, praying and counselling many. I was even asked to preach on Christmas day, and the day before the Lord gave me word-for-word the sermon, not at all about Christmas, but about Jesus, the Cross, and eternal life. One patient was dying, and I was certain the words reached her understanding.

Unfortunately my back was getting increasingly painful,

and I realised that I was not going to be able to cope with the hospital work much longer as it required a certain amount of strength to move the elderly patients. And the demonic attacks at night still had not left me so I was tired from lack of sleep. I took a lot of pain-killing tablets. After Christmas I stopped work with the thought of returning to Mike Costello and the Slade Green church for more help.

Hunting for help, in fact, was as much a drug as anything else I had taken. I wanted a good church and felt England promised the only one. I was tempted to attend a house church near Stuttgart where they sang many of the songs I had learned in England and worshipped in a lively way. There was something strange about the place, however. After I had been there a short time they prayed for me and I broke down under the power which hit me – it was intense and demonic. I discovered a spiritualist lived in the house and always stood in the doorway when meetings were going on. A witch lived next door and they worked together to destroy the church.

Their combined power was forced into me as the Christians were praying. I felt that dozens of men were pressing me into the floor, screaming in my ears . . . they were calling on all sorts of demons I didn't know were there. They refused to allow me to escape.

The church members kept me for the evening, praying until they tired, but kicked me out the following day, claiming I was a Satanist or some sort of devil. It was difficult to be called that in public. I determined to return to England for help.

Once more I packed the Volkswagen and drove to England.

The long journey and the extreme physical and psychological pressures gave me severe back pain – I could hardly operate the car's controls. Satan even sent a large animal – a deer – running into the path of the car and with blood all over the bonnet I dare not stop, knowing it was a satanist area. When I reported the incident the police perhaps not surprisingly, showed little interest.

I made one firm decision on returning to England: I would

not live with Peter and Mary but would stick with the
fellowship at Slade Green and work things out once and for
all. I wanted to be victorious.

Lacking the courage to 'live by faith' as I understood some
to do, I worked for a couple of days a week for CARE Trust
with Peter and the rest of my time was spent helping in the
Slade Green church. I began to see an important principle –
even though I knew there was a deeper root that still had to
come out, I nonetheless needed to reach out to others and
pray for them. I began to rejoice in being in a position to
increasingly give out what I had received. I was allowed to sit
in when Mike was counselling, and learnt a lot. God began to
give me pictures and sometimes a word which proved helpful
to others. As I developed a ministry, some of the sense of
fulfilment was robbed by the inner knowledge that I still had
further to go. A battle was raging within me, a clash of two
kingdoms – the kingdom of God and the kingdom of
darkness.

It was then that a friend from Germany arrived to stay
with me for six months. It was a great relief to have Beate
with me so that I could express myself freely in my native
tongue. Beate was lovely, she accepted me as I was and
always had a smile and an encouraging word. Free from the
language barrier I felt less insecure and isolated and found
comfort and companionship.

Still I was searching around for greater freedom. A
counselling centre in Felixstowe prayed for me; I attended
conferences and helped many other people, but all the while
I was crying out for help myself. Even at The Hyde the help I
needed seemed to have dried up.

Frank Marzullo and his wife came over from America and
I had a wonderful time with them, accompanying them to
Morecambe, near the Lake District, for a conference. It was
beautiful to be accepted and loved and cared for in a natural
way. They prayed a lot for me, and for my healing – it
brought relief for a time but my attacks always returned to
mystify them, and worry me. In fact my inclination was
towards evil instead of away from it. My nights continued to
be shattered by demonic visits when the fearsome fiends

would wake me up, pull the blankets off me, shake the bed
and rattle around the room as I froze in fear.

Mike reminded me of the previous advice I had never
completely followed – giving up all my family connections. I
looked at the family photographs, my father and mother, so
beautiful in their youth, myself as a child, newspaper
cuttings of my mother and father's athletic achievements – it
was too much to think of, getting rid of those memories. But
in a quiet way he was insistent and finally I agreed. They
were all burnt, or thrown away. My family memories had to
stay in my mind – there was no evidence anywhere else. One
other item had to be given away – the car. I looked at the
gleaming red of the faithful Volkswagen parked outside the
house. It had to go. I gave that to friends and refused any
money.

I had snapped the final links with the past. But if I
expected any sudden release I was disappointed. Instead I
walked around depressed, crying out to God: 'Where is this
road leading me?'

Receiving an invitation to a worship conference in the
Malvern area I was loaned Mike's car for the week. It was an
interesting conference but something of a strain since the
house in which I was staying seemed to be troubled with evil
spirits. I hardly slept thanks to my visiting apparitions.

On the way home an American serviceman drove into the
side of the car. Mike's car was extensively damaged and I
was taken to hospital with shock and my second case of
whiplash in my neck.

Not having slept during the week of the conference, the
accident was the last thing I could cope with. As I lay on the
X-ray table I felt myself sliding down a dark, slippery slope.
I felt guilty at having wrecked the car – even though the
accident was not my fault – and weeks of depression and
tears followed.

Healing and deliverance – the things I had craved ever
since becoming a Christian years before – seemed as far from
me as ever, but God was nearer than I thought. Dorothy, the
lovely lady I stayed with, looked after me, more and more
replacing my mother. Cooking, cleaning, caring and praying

– she did it all without complaining or criticising.

Occasionally light would shine through. Once I was running out of money and was in need of tights. I tried to live by faith and prayed about it. A few days later I received a package from an American friend – the whole parcel was full of tights in my size and style, with a bundle of other things I liked. I leaped round the house shouting: 'It works, it works!'

When Mike was asked to go to the Greater London Council to speak to the Christian Union he invited me to accompany him. I didn't suspect what it would lead to.

In the austere surroundings of County Hall on the opposite bank of the River Thames to the Houses of Parliament Mike spoke about deliverance and spiritual warfare.

One of the men at the meeting was married to a German woman and as we talked after the meeting he invited me to his home to meet her. I was delighted to accept, grasping at any chance to speak German and meet new people. I guess in the back of my mind there was also the hope that I would get fresh help.

A friendship developed with the family that was very enriching. They had five children, all loving the Lord, so it was a pleasure to be invited to return again and again. Mike and I were asked to the house group which met in their home and I was invited to spend a week with them. During this period I was visiting a doctor in London regularly. On his advice I applied to hospital for a thorough check-up on my back, and awaited a reply.

In July I went with other members of the Slade Green fellowship to Holy Trinity Church in Brompton, London, to listen to John Wimber, an American pastor who had been miraculously used in healing and deliverance work. He had begun his own work in America – the Vineyard Christian Fellowship – with a small number and it had grown to seven thousand people in a few years, since he had started to take God at his word and expect miracles to happen. I sat on the hard pew and listened. Something about the bearded teddy-bear of a man fascinated me. I couldn't explain it, but deep down I began to feel that my own personal victory would be bound up with this man and the message he was giving.

When the meeting ended, a conference was mentioned for October of the same year – John Wimber and members of his church in America would be back for Third Wave, ministering for a week in London. I knew I had to be there. But it was seventy pounds for the week's meetings and fares – more money than I had, especially since I was about to give up the work with CARE Trust because of my back pains. But when I finished my final day at CARE Trust I had a surprise. As a parting gift they paid for my attendance at the conference. It looked as if I could hear more of the work of the Holy Spirit and the power of the Lord Jesus through this servant of God, John Wimber.

One flaw appeared: the date came for my admission to hospital for the major check-up. The dates clashed. I had to make up my mind to which I gave priority – hospital, or the Third Wave conference; physical healing, or giving God the opportunity to heal me physically *and* spiritually. It was no contest. I knew Jesus wanted to heal and deliver me, so that was what I told the medical authorities when I cancelled my hospital appointment.

One Saturday a visit to London ended when I collapsed on the train journey home. As I faced the Sunday evening meeting I could cope no longer. The people of Slade Green had assured me of their love and desire to see me free, but I was so swamped by feelings of resentment and bitterness that I could receive nothing then. It was as though all the pain of a lifetime was converging within me.

I struggled desperately to be part of the worship. During communion I tried once more to reach out. Receiving communion should be a beautiful experience, but the darkness within me spoiled it. On this occasion, our pastor had suggested we share the bread and wine among ourselves, taking it to one another, following the guidance of the Holy Spirit. This was a special way of administering communion that we didn't practise very often. I served two ladies; returned to my seat and waited. No-one came to me. I felt hurt and isolated. I almost believed it was deliberate – such was my state of mind. My plight was noticed and Mike himself came with the bread and wine. But by this time the blackness had engulfed me completely. Even a call for healing didn't reach me and I walked out before the service ended. I ran mechanically, ignorant of the rain that soaked my clothes. I thought I would go mad if Jesus didn't free me soon. I felt totally rejected, not only by people, but also by God.

To reach my home, I had to cross a railway bridge. I paused for breath. A desire welled up inside me to jump in front of a train. I just wanted to die, to be released from my torment. My mind became obsessed with this idea, cutting out everything else.

A fast train approached the bridge and I prepared to jump. As I did something pulled me back. I looked round to see who was holding me. No-one was there. I was shocked. Was that the hand of the Lord again, protecting my life? Did he still love me? I cried out: 'God have mercy. Help me. Send someone. I am in great need. Jesus, help me.' My tears mingled with the raindrops and I went home to cry myself to sleep.

The following morning I was telephoned by Traudel – the German lady I had met as a result of that Greater London Council meeting. She asked me how I was, then came straight over to collect me. Despite having five children to look after Traudel somehow managed to create a single room for me and I was welcomed with open arms. For a few days I basked in the love of the Lord as it was revealed to me through this family.

During those days I heard of a conference in Croydon at a church pastored by John Edwards. Frank Hammond was there from America to speak on deliverance and spiritual warfare.

The first evening there were demonic manifestations from me when Frank did group deliverance. John Edwards came to me and from then on I had prayer and ministry for hours for up to three days a week, over a period of weeks. They prayed for healing, deliverance and inner healing. They anointed me with oil, prayed and fasted. Members of the fellowship even took days off work to pray for me. Again when at my lowest ebb I had been introduced to love and compassion of the highest order.

The deliverance sessions were sometimes incredibly hard going; my body was bleeding and aching after prayer, my muscles hard as stone and bruises appeared all over me.

During one session John prayed against the witchcraft which had been put into me by my family; for three hours they prayed, but it didn't go. Then they started to worship God, calling upon his angels and asking God to send angels to fight the demons. As John prayed I felt windows opening and angels entering – it was as if a wind were blowing and the room was filled with Holy presence. We all sensed it. And as the Holy presence entered the room demons left me, screaming and shouting – I was delivered. Peace and joy came, and for a few days I relaxed, unable to stand the physical pressure of more prayer, yet knowing it was not finished.

I still sensed something much deeper than anyone had dug yet. And the next event was nearly on me: the Third Wave conference with John Wimber. All my spiritual life I had been crying out for help, to be set free from that deep root within me. Would it happen during these coming days or not? I was tired of the wanderlust that had taken me all over Germany, to different parts of Britain, even to Africa for healing. There was no real reason for expecting anything out of the ordinary at Third Wave. I had been disappointed so many times. But deep within me was a feeling of hope. There was no vision; no word portrait; nothing but a simple faith that something miraculous was going to happen: God was about to intervene.

15

VICTORY

On the morning of 22 October, 1984, I took a taxi to the home of Ann and Perry, Californians who had befriended me some time before. Hearing that I was to attend the Wimber meetings they had invited me to stay at their home just off Baker Street in London.

Ironically the lovely house in a little road set back off the busy Marylebone High Street was not far from the former site of London Bible College. The college had by now moved out to Northwood in Middlesex but the building looked very little different. My journey was to end not far from where it had started. Ann welcomed me to the house and showed me to my room – a third-floor bedroom with its own bathroom, delicately decorated in pastel shades. It was lovely. The beauty of it didn't really impress me, however. I was too keyed-up with anxiety over what lay ahead. We had coffee and then called another taxi for the long-awaited journey to Westminster Central Hall where the meetings were to be held.

We walked up the staircase into the lobby – a huge area with doors going into the main hall. Ann took me to a desk where we had to register for the week. A short queue delayed us, then we were invested with literature and made our way into the main arena, sitting downstairs in the middle of the central row of seats.

Singing started... then John Wimber appeared on the platform which stretched across most of the front of the hall. In his blue pullover and white trousers he looked like a doctor on holiday. But his smile warmed my heart and his conversational approach helped. I began to drink in his

words... he talked of his own pilgrimage and discovery of
God's power; of healing; of the constant battle between God
and Satan and the victories there were waiting for Christians.

When he finished there was a hush as he introduced the
time for ministry. The two thousand or so people packing
the hall, upstairs and down, waited to see what God was
going to do. Wimber didn't bully, cajole, or coax us into
doing anything, he simply paced the platform waiting and
watching...

People began to pray for each other. Things started to
happen. Occasionally John Wimber or one of his team
would use a word of knowledge to identify a need in the
audience and call someone out for prayer. Several people, in
fact, had made their way to the front when a team member
said softly into the microphone: 'A lady with serious sinus
disease needs help.'

I pricked up my ears. I had been having sinus trouble for
years and in the last few weeks it had got worse. I wasn't
going to move, however. But the message continued... He
gave my age – thirty-seven – identified the areas of pain, and
several other personal things which he couldn't have known.

I knew God was moving. I couldn't resist. I stood, and
struggled past the row of people praying until I reached the
aisle. I turned and went to the platform, climbing a few small
steps to reach John Wimber. I was hot and trembling, afraid
of what might happen. He smiled. 'I'm the sinus,' was all I
could think of to say. With those words it began: a group of
people stood around me and suddenly I began to manifest,
but healing power did not flow into me as I had hoped,
instead demonic power flowed out. I collapsed on to the
floor as the knot of prayers closed in and fervently lifted me
up to God.

They prayed for probably about half-an-hour; then the
clock identified the time as ten p.m. and we had to leave the
hall.

Ann rushed up to me and led me to a taxi for the journey
home. Once there we had a drink and I went to bed. The pain
in my head was excruciating; the evil presence which had
always haunted my sleep returned in force; and I lay on the

bed in an agony of conscience, desperately hoping that something would happen the next day.

Ann and I arrived early for the next morning's session. We sat near the front on the left. 'How are you today?' one of the team asked, recognising me. I told them my pain was worse but that I believed it was something far more sinister than the sinus trouble – a real root of evil needed identifying.

Some members of the team felt an inward assurance that I was correct and began praying for me again. For two hours they prayed. Fortunately they were gathered at the front of the hall between the platform and the first seats – not on the actual platform itself, so at least I wasn't too embarrassed.

When the prayers ended I was able to enjoy the worship – a holy atmosphere seemed to have settled over the whole place. But as I entered into it more I began to feel uneasy, something was reacting and bringing a spirit of hatred to the atmosphere. 'Lord,' I cried, 'is it possible that I am so bound that I can't even enjoy the worship?'

I wanted to run from the hall or shout at them to stop. My arms felt like iron – moulded to my sides, and my whole body seemed to be chained. I called on God to deliver me. Darkness and light were using me as a battleground again. It was a feeling that persisted through the afternoon and evening meetings but I was determined not to give in. Ann graciously stood by me and took me home for another sleepless, pain-racked night.

Wednesday morning dawned and with it came the most crucial experience in all my life. As we arrived at the Central Hall and made our way to the same front seats – almost ours by right now – I felt different.

The atmosphere was supercharged with an increasing feeling of holiness. Suddenly I began to weep. A feeling of dirtiness and blackness seemed to well up from inside me and became so strong that I could not hold back the tears. I wanted to be clean.

As the tears coursed down my face, one of the team members, Walter Dettart, came to me. Immediately he began to challenge a demon of Satan-worship within me. As soon as he did so I was catapulted from my chair to the front of the stage, screaming, kicking and biting anyone near me and completely losing control of myself. The demons within me tossed me backwards and forwards. As Walter prayed I lapsed into a state of unconsciousness but, when others told me of my actions afterwards, I was glad I couldn't see. It sounded dreadful.

Eventually I came to lying on the floor with a group of men holding me down and attempting to calm me. I was shocked.

Now I was certain I was insane. This, I reckoned, must be the end. One of the helpers prayed continuously 'Peace be with you', and as he continued to recite the words I felt them taking hold of my frenetic spirit and soothing it. Gradually I began to realise what had happened. As I did so the enormity of it hit me. 'These people will believe I am not normal. They will leave me or send me to hospital,' I thought. An even worse idea came to my mind: 'I am a foreigner – they will send me back to Germany without any spiritual help.'

All of a sudden a man sat down on the floor beside me, put his arm round me and placed his face very close to mine. I could almost feel his heart of love. He had black hair and warm-looking eyes but his voice was even more warm and comforting: 'Don't worry and don't be afraid. You will be set free. Everything will be all right. Jesus loves you and he is in control. Can you hear me?'

I had heard, but the words sounded so beautiful and good I said: 'No', and listened as he repeated them exactly.

A surge of hope was injected into me and peace took over. As I looked around the man had gone, and when I asked the team gathered all round me they said they had not seen anyone of that description. They had just felt something happen to me.

My heart leapt. It must have been an angel – an incredible experience. The Lord must still love me to allow something so beautiful to happen. Walter then assured me he would select a special team to minister me.

By now it was midday and when Ann and I arrived home I showered, changed and ate as if in a dream world. I was so dreamy I hardly remember the afternoon meeting – it seemed to drift by in a haze.

All I could think of now was how and when would I be set free? There was room for no other thoughts. John Wimber had earlier given an illustration of how God had occasionally spoken to him using banners – sorts of flags with words on them. In my blunt way I told God that there was no difference between John Wimber and me – I wanted a banner to tell me when to expect freedom! With hindsight it seemed a megalomaniac challenge, but I was desperate.

And Jesus answered! As I sat soaking up the singing and worship early in the evening meeting I saw a banner with the word 'Tomorrow' on it in bold letters. It was very clear and, despite my initial disbelief, remained in front of my eyes for some time.

Of course my natural stupidity and enthusiasm took over and I went forward for prayer at the end of the meeting. It was a disaster! Different people prayed for me in a side room but seemed powerless. The team praying did not know my case history and some of the prayers were well meant but drove me deeper into myself. I should not have gone forward – it was not my time. The banner had said 'Tomorrow'. I was stunned, feeling nothing emotionally or spiritually. People came and hugged me and said nice things but little of it reached me. When Ann and I returned home I dropped down on the large, comfortable bed and sobbed into the quilt. All night I was awake praying, crying, and calling on God for mercy.

It must have been habit that helped me shower and dress in the morning, but a cup of coffee later we were en route for Westminster Central Hall once more – Thursday, with the conference week half over. What I did not know was that kind Walter had realised my plight and late the previous evening had called a small group together to pray, fast and wrestle with God on my behalf.

As the taxi deposited us at the hall and we took our seats at the front I was short on confidence. My prayers throughout the night had been for forgiveness . . . I had listed everyone I

could remember wronging, every item I could recall that
might block my progress to God and pleaded for forgiveness
with them all. At one time I had considered walking upstairs
to the roof garden and throwing myself off the surrounding
wall into the street four storeys below. That would have
solved everything. But I could not move from my bedroom.
Jesus was very near, carrying me through the night.

Now I was alive, in the hall, with a minimal faith but
conscious in a strange way of Jesus holding my hand.

As the meeting got under way expectancy surged through
me in increasing tides. I could sense the power in the service
but was more occupied with myself, determined to prevent
myself doing anything strange in public.

It was before the afternoon meeting that Walter came and
spoke to me. He enquired whether I was ready to be prayed
for again and suggested a small room at the back of the main
hall so that I would not need to fear embarrassment.

It was kind – but I was still terrified. Walter introduced me
to Jim McDonough from California and as I looked at him I
could sense the love and compassion radiating from him. I
knew now that the team were ready to help me: I had the
promise from God that it would be today; and I felt Jim was
someone in whom I could put my trust.

As soon as they began to pray I was thrown to the floor.
The rest is a blur in my mind. I know some of the men were
holding me, but I managed to struggle from their grip and
smash my head into the wall. It was dreadfully painful and
they had to pray for that injury before continuing with the
deliverance.

As they prayed I felt hurts from the past being smoothed
away in forgiveness ... it was as if many bleeding wounds
were drying out and the scars wiped away. Just as I was
dedicated to Satan as a baby and every part of my body had
been touched, they anointed my whole body with oil and
rededicated me to Jesus – the women praying over the more
intimate parts of my body. It seemed to take hours but they
were not hurrying. Heat seemed to scorch my flesh as they
touched it, burning away the evil from the past.

The ministry had started at four in the afternoon, and

because the authorities insisted the hall was vacated at ten
p.m., the team had contacted the minister at St Mark's
Church in Kennington, London, and he had agreed to put a
room at our disposal for as long as necessary. They felt it
would take longer and were determined to see me through. I
was put into a taxi with three of the team while others hailed
another cab and followed us to the church.

There seemed to be no break, for ministry resumed as
soon as we arrived. By now my body was black and blue with
bruises which were swollen and sore – it looked as if I had
been beaten, not prayed for. I didn't care. I knew that this
time the Devil was on the run and we were reaching the roots
of my life-time of servitude to Satan. The struggle was tough
and took as much out of the willing faithful team as it did
from me. Jim lost his voice at times because of the constant
praying and commanding the demons to go.

It was a time of awful contrasts... sometimes I felt the
warmth of God eating away my past... at other times I
wanted to reach out and strangle Jim and Walter, they
seemed too kind and holy and I was locked in darkness.

When they broke to rest for five minutes I asked Jim about
an odd sentence I had picked up during the evening. I had
heard him say to someone: 'Look, this is the answer to our
prophecy.' He explained that in California months before, as
they were praying about their trip to London, God had told
them that during the week they would have to minister to a
lady and cast out a high priest of the occult from her. They
had recognised that prophecy as coming true in me.

Shocked as I was by those words I was excited that Jesus
had begun to prepare them for my deliverance half-way
across the world. My freedom was so important to Jesus.
And I was also reassured that I had not been on my own in
my struggle. In fact, God has used quite a few Christians on
my way to freedom.

I had fresh hope as they began to pray again. Now I was
confident that I was not going mad, neither was suicide the
answer – but a life of freedom and light. As the ministry
continued I felt as if I were receding into a picture-frame,
part of a moving portrait of my past. I saw myself as a little

girl of four behind a beige curtain being married to Satan. Jim told me to speak it out and break its power by bringing it into the open. Never. I couldn't. Again and again he implored me to tell what I was seeing.

But the realisation of what it meant was gripping me as I relived those frightful moments – moments I was seeing and understanding for the first time, since I was too small to understand before. I was in agony. Jim kept begging to know, but it was too horrible to speak of. Then Jim started to weep. He knelt on the floor beside me, sobbing; Walter joined him, and soon the whole team was crying before the Lord on my behalf.

I broke. Great gulps dragged the tears from me, huge racking sobs, and Jim began to tell me what I was seeing. He drew the picture for me and I simply sobbed out the words he was speaking after him, confirming the dreadful scenes.

They allowed me time to weep and scream all my hurts and feelings into the open. As I lay exhausted they began to speak to the demons, ordering them to leave me. It was like going through hell itself. If the previous few hours had been torment this was worse. And yet despite it all I knew the Lord was at work and he was in control. It was not a bad dream but painful reality.

'In the Name of Jesus out,' Jim demanded again and again, and more and more demons would wrench themselves free from me and disappear. Well after midnight Jim and Walter decided to give me a rest. With powerful authority which is given by an anointing of the Holy Spirit the remaining demons were bound. I was told to rest and sleep.

Back where I was staying, I stumbled up the stairs to my room after yet another taxi ride, feeling as if an army had walked all over me. It was all I could do to sink into the warmth of a bath and crawl under the soft quilt into the bed. My mind was a turmoil of activity as I tried to sleep . . . But sleep came, mixed with a digest of the events of the night.

Friday morning dawned with my aching limbs reluctantly obeying my wishes and carrying me downstairs to Ann and a drink of coffee.

We arrived at the hall early – in time for the pre-service

worship time. Jim saw me as soon as I arrived and instructed me to enjoy the meeting as much as I was able before we went to the room for prayer. I felt freer already and much more ready to enjoy the worship... things had obviously been accomplished.

Just before John Wimber began to preach, the team took me into the ante-room and began to minister to me. At first I was a little shocked – there were so many more people than the night before. But I realised I had to trust them and recognised God's hand in it all. It led to one unusual incident: a lady from Colorado was with us; she had been born in Austria and spoke German. Amazingly as she prayed and ordered demons out they seemed to obey much quicker when addressed in German. I can't explain it.

John Wimber came in at one point – an indication of how long we had been praying since he had obviously finished preaching – and open to the Lord's leading, he advised the team how to continue ministering. The ground that had been won the previous night gave the team a solid foothold and they dug deeper with their prayers until the very root of the evil that had assailed me for thirty-seven years was prised out.

At last it was over.

For some hours I felt nothing but total emptiness. Walter stayed with me for some time speaking encouragement and peace.

I knew I was free. Deliverance had taken place. Jesus had heard my cries and answered my prayers. He had set me free. The wonder of that moment is hard to describe – I walked around, constantly repeating the same prayer: 'Thank you Jesus – I love you Lord – thank you.'

What a joy to go to the evening meeting! No fear of manifestations. No fear at all, only peace – a peace that passes understanding and only Jesus can give (Philippians 4:7). Oh, how I enjoyed the worship. It was miraculous for me. I could pray and sing in other tongues, there were no hindrances or disturbances. My hands were raised – I could kneel down and lose myself in the presence of the Lord.

John stood to give his talk and, as I saw him on the

platform just a few feet away, everything drifted out of my vision. I was struck by the Holy Spirit, my hands and arms rooted to my side, unable to move, speak or even see as a glorious, blissful experience took me over for about an hour.

As I sat I saw Jesus coming nearer and nearer... I saw myself as a little girl and Jesus bowing down to pick me up. His strong arms lifted me and he sat down, putting me on his lap and wrapping his arms around me. The most beautiful hug encompassed me. Time and space lost all meaning. I wanted it to go on for ever. I was loved by my Lord – in his arms!

I felt something cleansing me... dirt and filth falling off. Memories that had haunted me for years came and went, but they went beautifully blessed and healed.

The picture dimmed and then came back into focus. Now I was a baby, naked and held by the Father. He held me with outstretched arms under a stream of blood from his Son and the blood washed me clean. It didn't feel like washing or showering, it felt like a lovely warm bath.

Just as I felt warm and clean all over the Father drew me close to his chest and stroked me. Divine love was poured into my whole being. I knew without a doubt that the wickedness that had dogged my foosteps all my life was broken. Peace deeper than any understanding was within and around me.

I spent the night and Saturday morning before the Lord in my bedroom with the same pictures often recurring – myself as a little girl safe in the arms of Jesus and at the chest of the Father. Even deeper peace floated through my inner being as more and more healing seemed to go on. The beauty of it enraptured me all Saturday and I don't even remember eating before going to the evening meeting – the final meeting for the Wimber team.

All I know is that when I glanced in the mirror to arrange my clothes before leaving the room I was surprised by what I saw: there was something different about me. The freedom showed, and with it peace, joy, relaxation and light.

It was evident also when I walked into the hall. One of the team grabbed my hand and led me to the other members showing them the difference in my appearance. One of them hugged me and said about five times 'You are wonderful', and for the first time I felt able to take the words, praise God for them and rejoice in them.

The whole evening was a dream. I praised, worshipped, praised God in tongues, and there were no disturbances and no fear of what I might do next.

I couldn't praise God enough.

John Wimber preached in a powerful way. At one point he said God had given him a word for Britain: 'Give me back my church.' God whispered into my praising heart that it was a word for my own country too – Germany. He had finally won me back. He wanted my all. And he wanted to take me where he would have me go.

As usual when he finished preaching John paused and then encouraged people to sense what the Holy Spirit wanted. People began to pray for each other. Jim and members of the team came across to me, praying. I didn't open my eyes: I wanted so much to concentrate on Jesus. But one sentence of a prayer brought the tears to my eyes. 'Lord Jesus, give Gabriele back all the years Satan has taken away from her.'

I felt ten years younger, keenly looking to the future and what God wanted me to do.

I was told to get involved with the meeting. 'Minister to others,' Walter said.

Shy and shaky I laid my hands on someone and prayed. It was a blind man I had got to know a little during the week.

Deep inside I felt an inner voice telling me: 'This man first needs an inner healing before he can be physically healed. The hurt within him is greater than the physical blindness. Kneel before him and kiss his eyes.'

It was too much for me. I must have misunderstood. Who was I to do something like that? I struggled with the Lord, but the command came again: 'Kiss his eyes.' I had never kissed a man before – and now this! Yet because of all the Lord had done for me I could not refuse. I mentioned the feeling to one of the team. He simply told me to be obedient.

I asked the man if he minded. He said: 'No.' As soon as I

knelt and touched his eyes with my lips the power of God hit us. I felt and knew something was happening to the man – and to myself. He was sixty-five and five years previously someone had thrown acid in his face, blinding him. We knew something happened inside Arthur (that was his name) even though he walked out still blind. I met him a year later and called out. He responded: 'Gabriele – the one who kissed my eyes,' and gave me a big hug.

For me that experience was a fresh calling from God. Years before he had given me a love for him and a desire to serve him. Now I could do it. A new life had just begun. I might have been sold to Satan – but Jesus had bought me back through his precious blood shed at Calvary. And now he had delivered me – delivered me to declare!

16

CONCLUSION

In July 1985 – nine months after the Lord had so graciously delivered me from the occult roots which had bound me for thirty-seven years – my mother became a Christian.

The Lord had sent me back to Asperg to visit her and every night I prayed by her bedside. One night she joined me in prayer, asking for forgiveness, and inviting Jesus Christ into her life. It was not easy – for mother, or myself – but that is her testimony, and another story.

Reconciliation is miraculous, both between an individual and Christ and between a mother and child. I experienced both.

In February 1986 – while I was writing this final chapter, in fact – I received a phone call to tell me that my mother had died. Despite my grief at the loss there was the joy that she was with the Lord. Sadly, but in a way fortunately, I became increasingly aware that her death in Christ had completed my freedom. I praise God that Jesus has taken away my responsibility for her, physically and spiritually. Truly, his ways are not our ways.

Don't put this book down with the illusion that everything is over. Salvation means wholeness – body, soul and spirit, and this is a process which needs time. I have discovered three truths which have helped me:

One is that we have an enemy, Satan, who is real. I have begun to understand his tactics – it is the only way to begin to fight back.

The second is that we have an ally – the Lord Jesus Christ. What he has done, and continues to do through the presence of his Holy Spirit, brings victory.

The third truth – and often the most difficult to grasp – is that I have a part to play in God's plans. Yesterday's miracles and victories encourage me as I face the challenge of today's battle. The battle goes on, but Satan is a defeated foe! I am increasingly aware that my deliverance and healing was not just for my own benefit; God allowed the events of this book to happen to me so that the experiences I went through would enable me to understand, and be able to minister to others. No teaching is as valuable as experience.

The Lord is using me more and more in the deliverance ministry, as well as in the ministries of healing and inner healing. I have been able to return to Germany on a number of occasions to take the good news that Jesus not only wants to save, but to set free – to deliver from demonic bondage. Jesus sends us out to preach, heal and cast out demons – what a great joy to know that despite my pathway he has allowed me the privilege of using his own precious name to oppose the powers of darkness and cause demons to flee.

This book is a humble attempt to document my own experiences. I realise that for some the reading of it will raise more questions than it provides answers. My prayer is that those with needs similar to my own will encounter, as I did, the great God of our salvation.

Victory is possible through the Lord Jesus Christ, for me and for you!